Jason

WEREWOLVES
OF MONTPELLIER

FANTAGRAPHICS BOOKS

ALSO BY JASON:

Almost Silent
(collecting The Living and the Dead,
Meow, Baby!, Tell Me Something, and
You Can't Get There From Here)
Hey, Wait…
I Killed Adolf Hitler
The Last Musketeer
The Living and the Dead
The Left Bank Gang
Low Moon
Pocket Full of Rain
Sshhhh!
Tell Me Something
What I Did
(collecting Hey, Wait…,
The Iron Wagon, and Sshhhh!)
Why Are You Doing This?

FANTAGRAPHICS BOOKS
7563 Lake City Way NE, Seattle WA 98115

Translated by Kim Thompson
Designed by Jason and Covey
Production and lettering by Paul Baresh
Associate Publisher: Eric Reynolds
Published by Gary Groth and Kim Thompson

Special thanks to Jérôme Martineau
at Editions de Tournon-Carabas.

To receive a free catalog of comics, call 1-800-657-1100 or
write us at Fantagraphics Books, 7563 Lake City Way NE,
Seattle, WA 98115.

Distributed in the U.S. by W.W. Norton and Company, Inc.
(212-354-5500)
Distributed in Canada by Canadian Manda Group
(416-516-0911)
Distributed in the United Kingdom by Turnaround
Distribution (208-829-3009)
Distributed to the comics market by Diamond Comic
Distributors, Inc. (410-560-7100)

Visit the website for The Beguiling, where Jason's original
artwork can be purchased: www.beguiling.com
Visit the Fantagraphics website: www.fantagraphics.com

First printing: May, 2010

ISBN: 978-1-60699-359-0

Printed in China

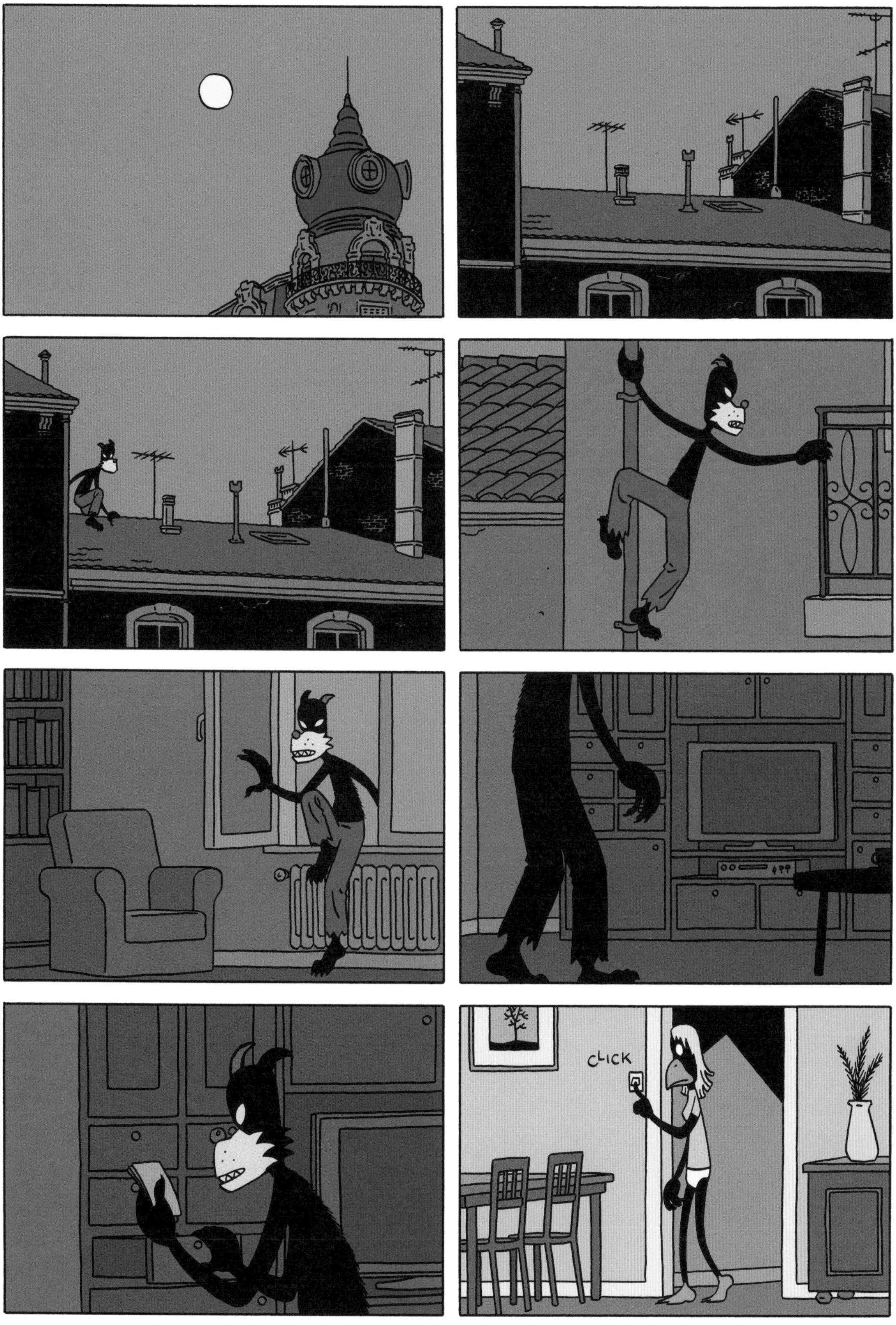
CLICK

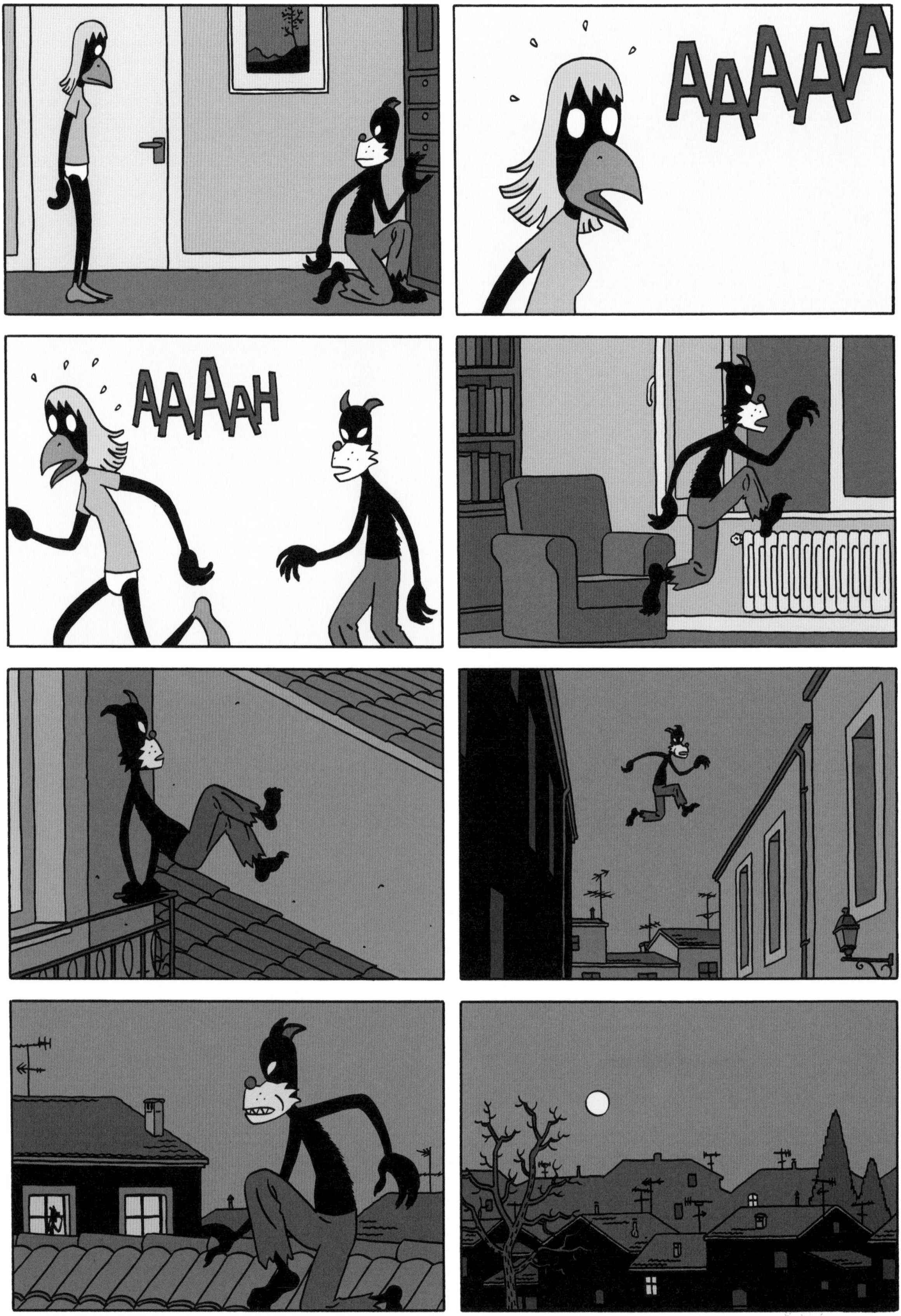
AAAAA
AAAAH

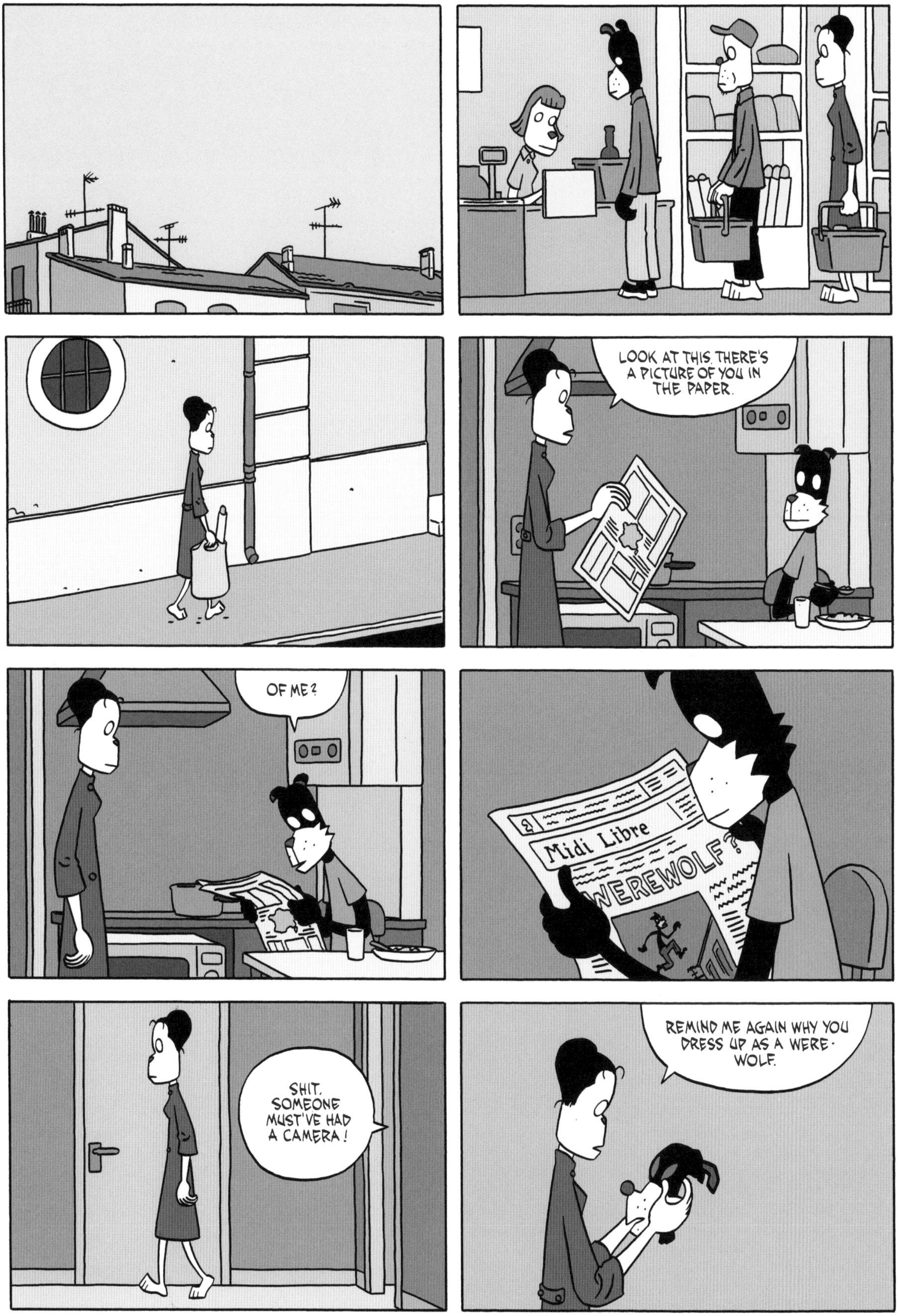
LOOK AT THIS. THERE'S A PICTURE OF YOU IN THE PAPER.
OF ME?
Midi Libre
WEREWOLF?
SHIT. SOMEONE MUST'VE HAD A CAMERA!
REMIND ME AGAIN WHY YOU DRESS UP AS A WERE-WOLF.

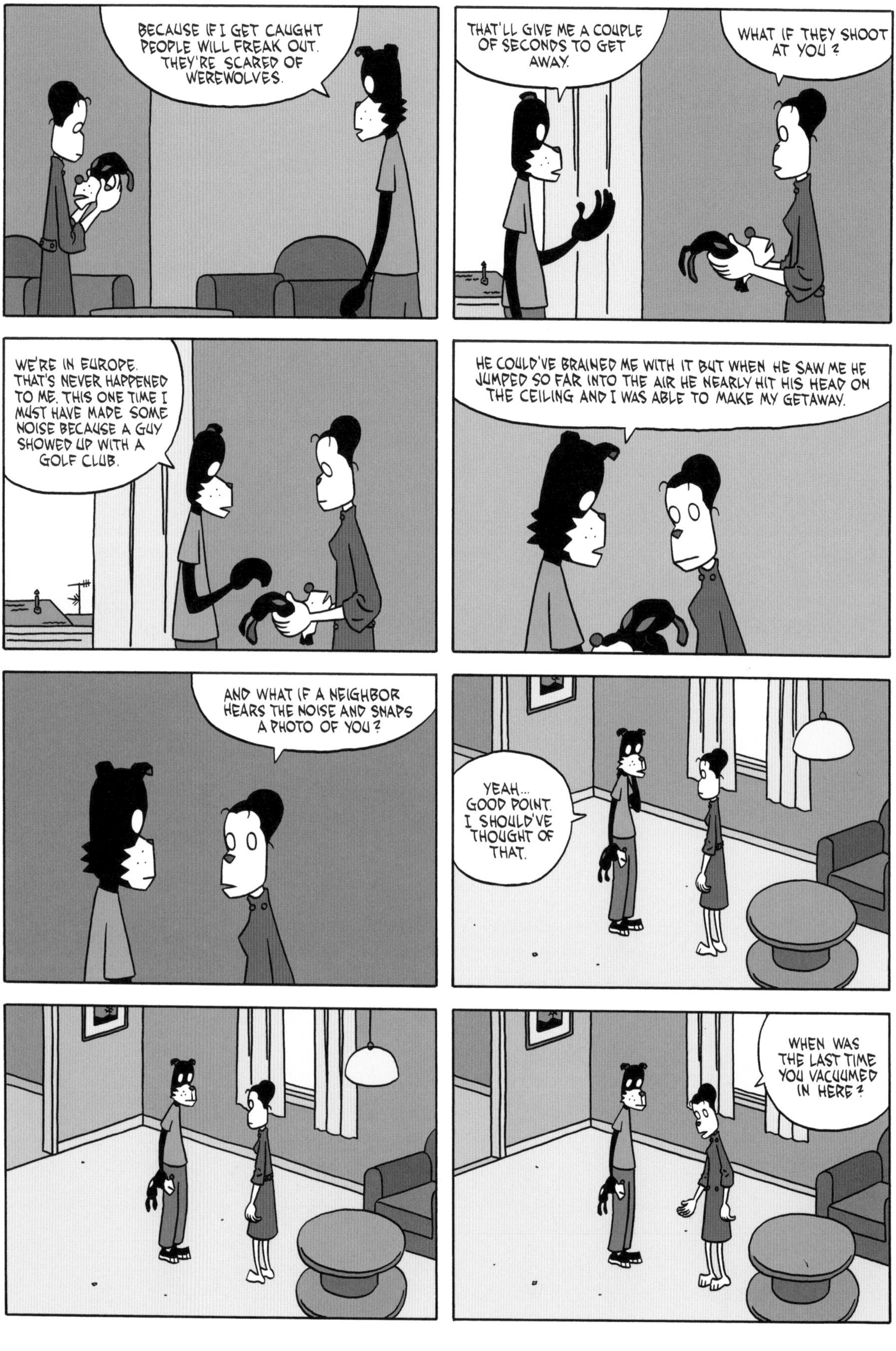
BECAUSE IF I GET CAUGHT PEOPLE WILL FREAK OUT. THEY'RE SCARED OF WEREWOLVES.
THAT'LL GIVE ME A COUPLE OF SECONDS TO GET AWAY.
WHAT IF THEY SHOOT AT YOU?
WE'RE IN EUROPE. THAT'S NEVER HAPPENED TO ME. THIS ONE TIME I MUST HAVE MADE SOME NOISE BECAUSE A GUY SHOWED UP WITH A GOLF CLUB.
HE COULD'VE BRAINED ME WITH IT BUT WHEN HE SAW ME HE JUMPED SO FAR INTO THE AIR HE NEARLY HIT HIS HEAD ON THE CEILING AND I WAS ABLE TO MAKE MY GETAWAY.
AND WHAT IF A NEIGHBOR HEARS THE NOISE AND SNAPS A PHOTO OF YOU?
YEAH... GOOD POINT. I SHOULD'VE THOUGHT OF THAT.
WHEN WAS THE LAST TIME YOU VACUUMED IN HERE?

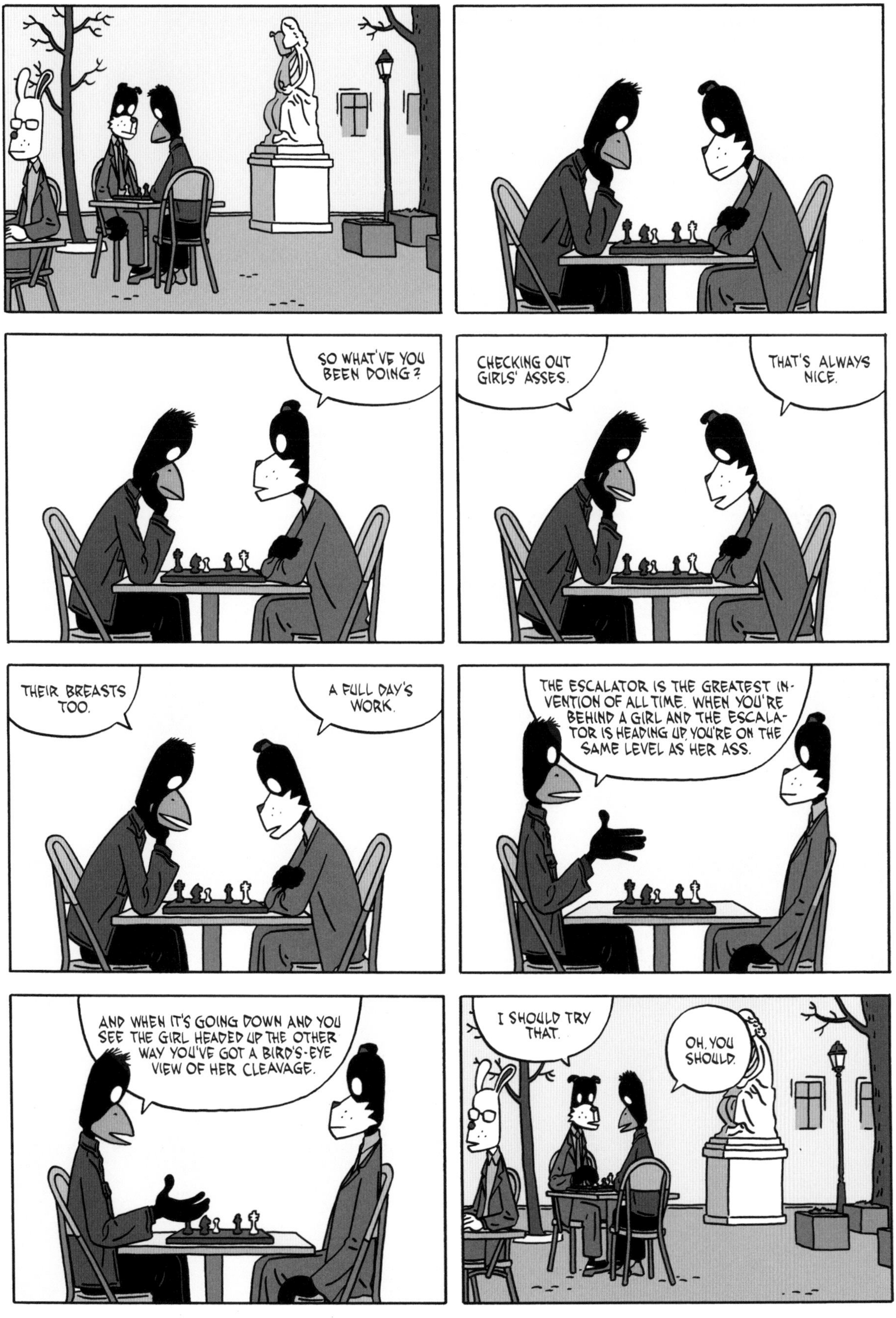
SO WHAT'VE YOU BEEN DOING?
CHECKING OUT GIRLS' ASSES.
THAT'S ALWAYS NICE.
THEIR BREASTS TOO.
A FULL DAY'S WORK.
THE ESCALATOR IS THE GREATEST INVENTION OF ALL TIME. WHEN YOU'RE BEHIND A GIRL AND THE ESCALATOR IS HEADING UP, YOU'RE ON THE SAME LEVEL AS HER ASS.
AND WHEN IT'S GOING DOWN AND YOU SEE THE GIRL HEADED UP THE OTHER WAY YOU'VE GOT A BIRD'S-EYE VIEW OF HER CLEAVAGE.
I SHOULD TRY THAT.
OH, YOU SHOULD.

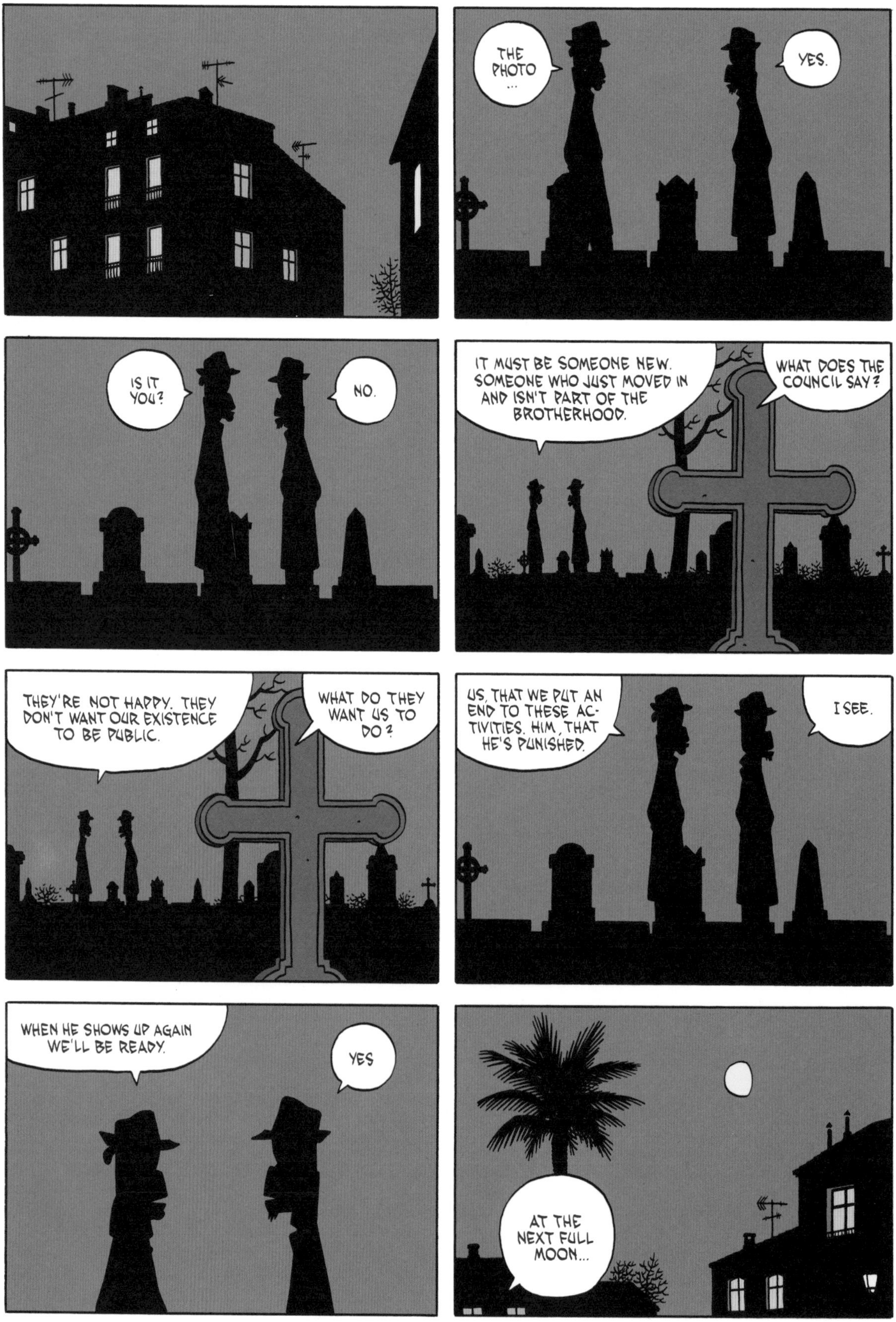
THE PHOTO ...
YES.
IS IT YOU?
NO.
IT MUST BE SOMEONE NEW. SOMEONE WHO JUST MOVED IN AND ISN'T PART OF THE BROTHERHOOD.
WHAT DOES THE COUNCIL SAY?
THEY'RE NOT HAPPY. THEY DON'T WANT OUR EXISTENCE TO BE PUBLIC.
WHAT DO THEY WANT US TO DO?
US, THAT WE PUT AN END TO THESE ACTIVITIES. HIM, THAT HE'S PUNISHED.
I SEE.
WHEN HE SHOWS UP AGAIN WE'LL BE READY.
YES
AT THE NEXT FULL MOON...

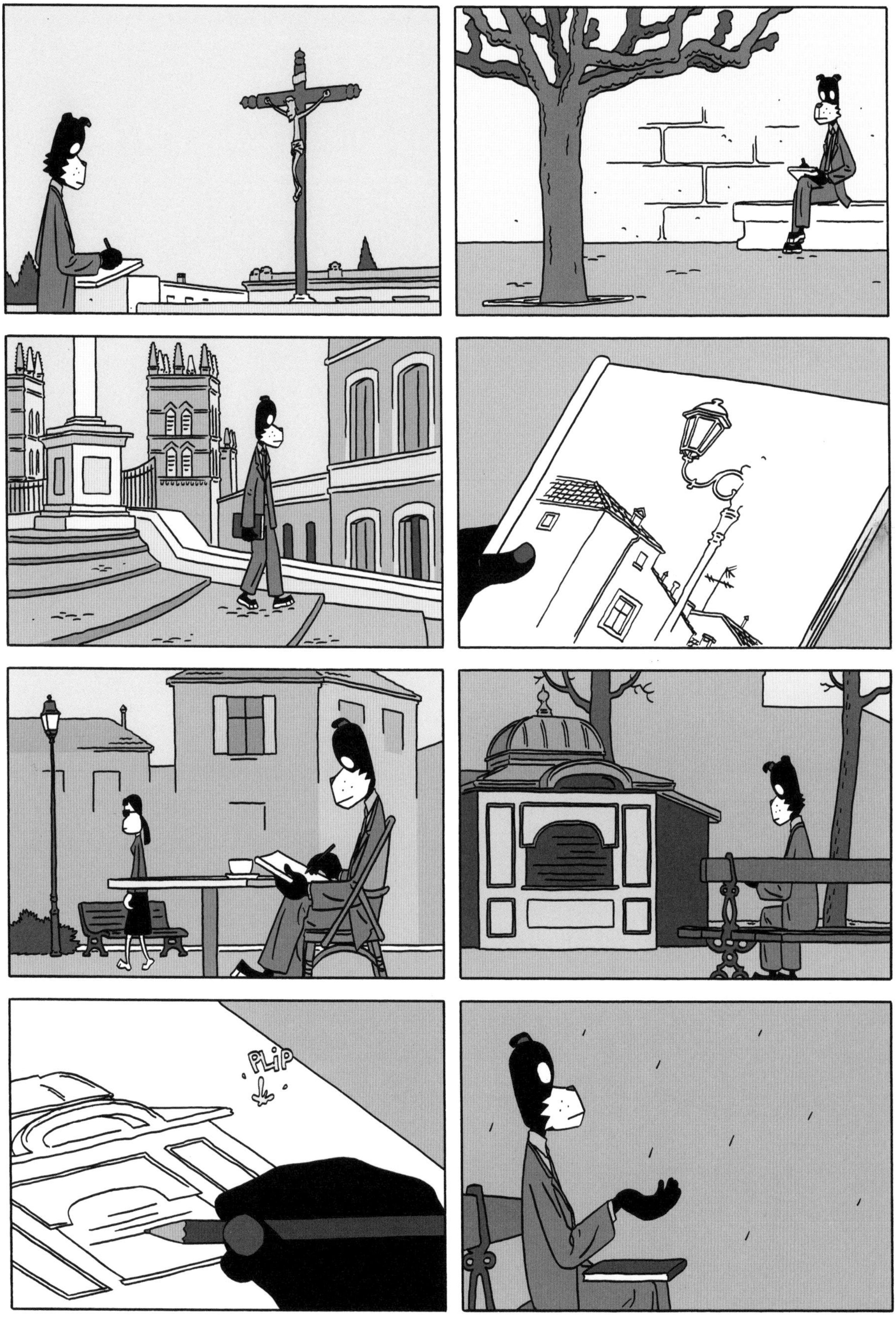
PLIP

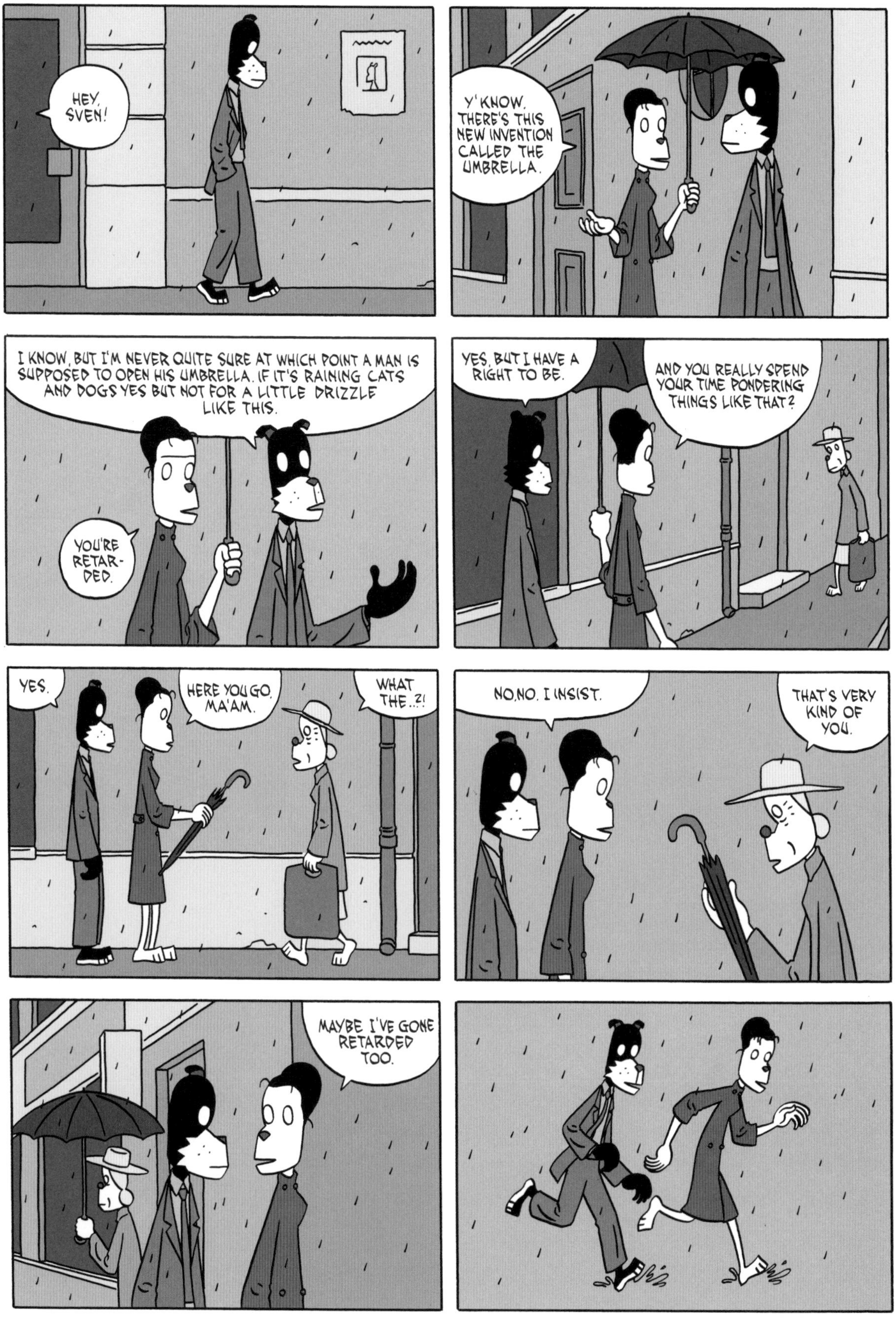
HEY, SVEN!
Y'KNOW, THERE'S THIS NEW INVENTION CALLED THE UMBRELLA.
I KNOW, BUT I'M NEVER QUITE SURE AT WHICH POINT A MAN IS SUPPOSED TO OPEN HIS UMBRELLA. IF IT'S RAINING CATS AND DOGS YES BUT NOT FOR A LITTLE DRIZZLE LIKE THIS.
YOU'RE RETAR-DED.
AND YOU REALLY SPEND YOUR TIME PONDERING THINGS LIKE THAT?
YES, BUT I HAVE A RIGHT TO BE.
YES.
HERE YOU GO, MA'AM.
WHAT THE...?!
NO,NO. I INSIST.
THAT'S VERY KIND OF YOU.
MAYBE I'VE GONE RETARDED TOO.

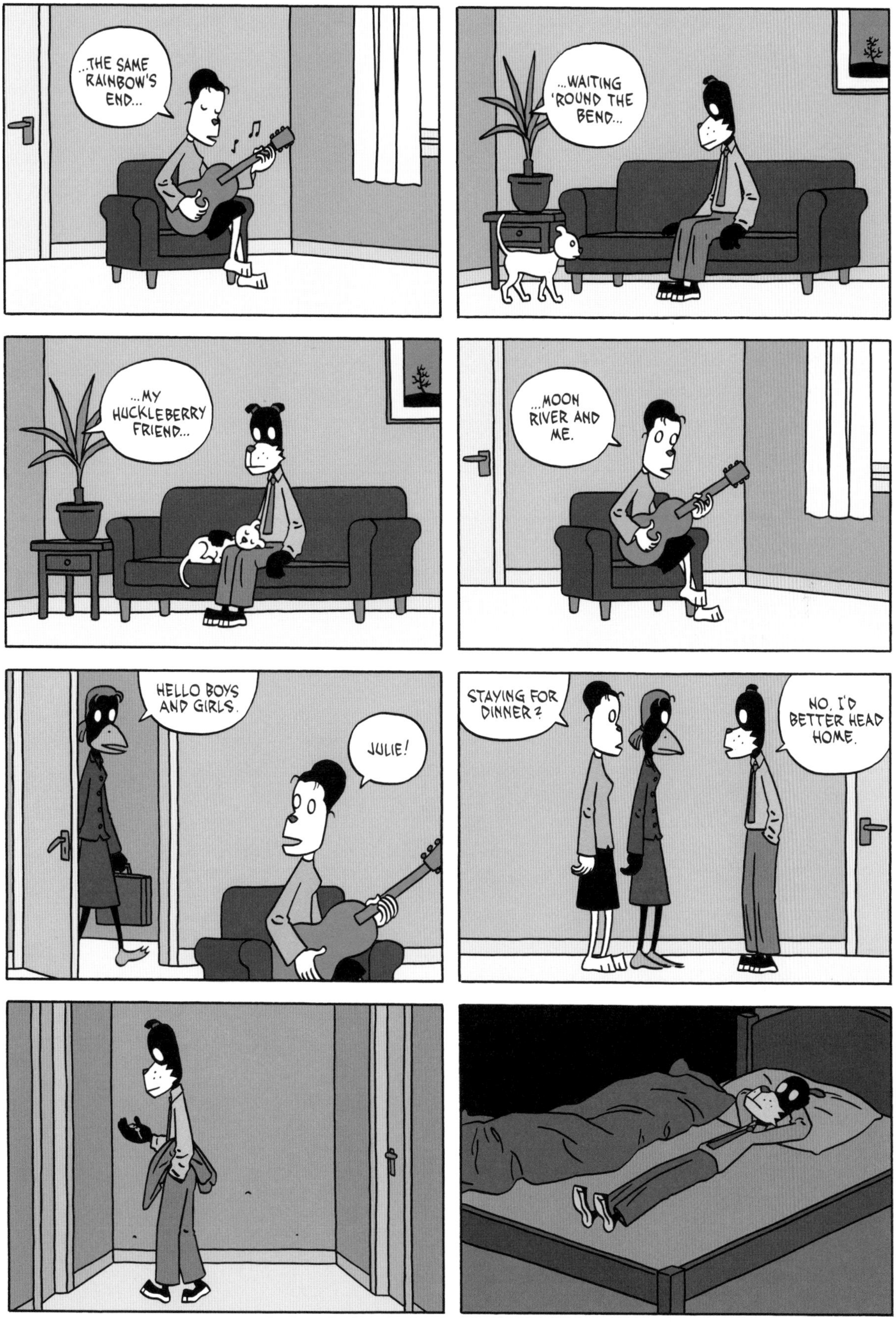
...THE SAME RAINBOW'S END...
...WAITING 'ROUND THE BEND...
...MY HUCKLEBERRY FRIEND...
...MOON RIVER AND ME.
HELLO BOYS AND GIRLS.
JULIE!
STAYING FOR DINNER?
NO, I'D BETTER HEAD HOME.

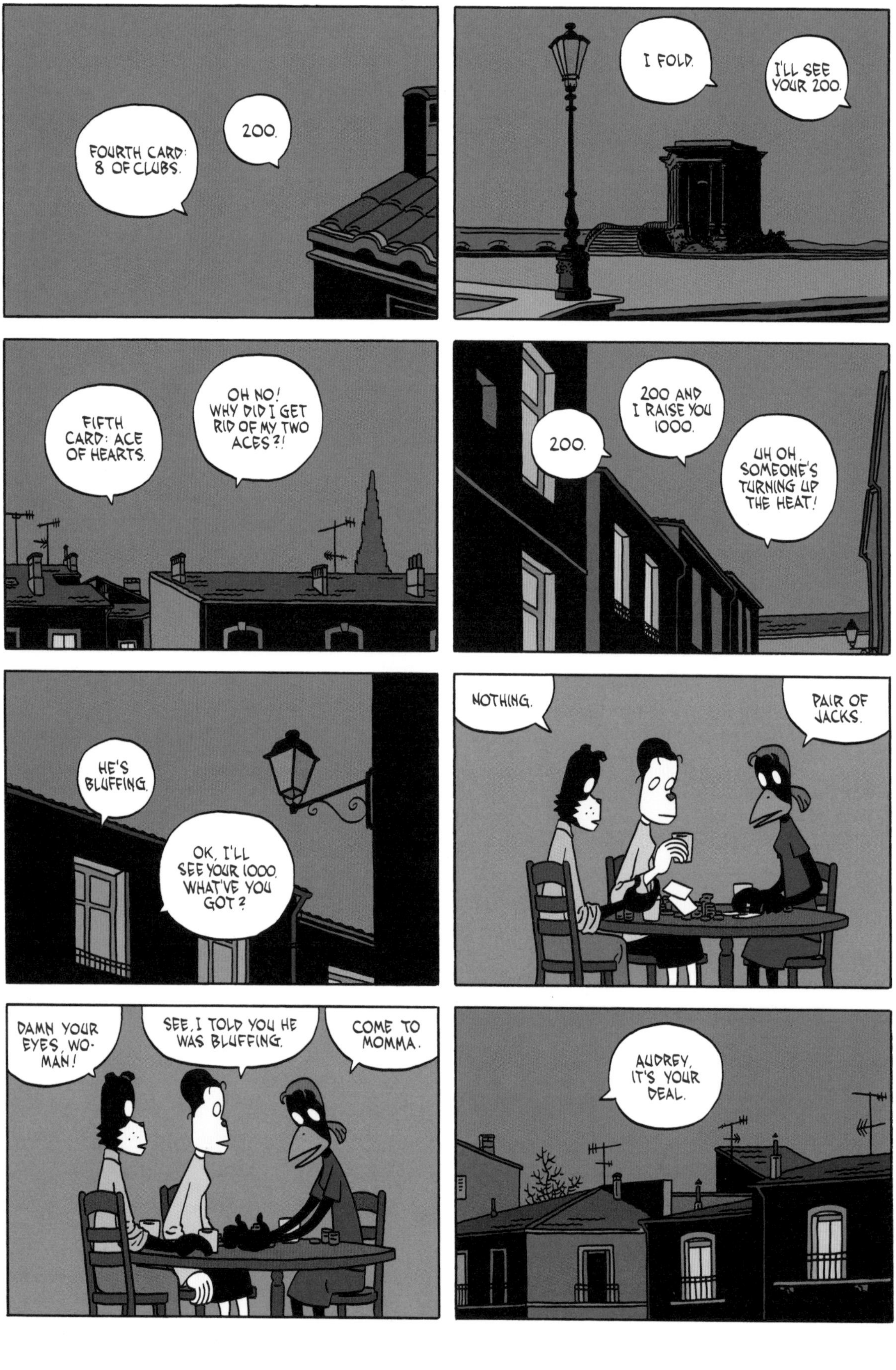
FOURTH CARD: 8 OF CLUBS.
200.
I FOLD.
I'LL SEE YOUR 200.
FIFTH CARD: ACE OF HEARTS.
OH NO! WHY DID I GET RID OF MY TWO ACES?!
200.
200 AND I RAISE YOU 1000.
UH OH. SOMEONE'S TURNING UP THE HEAT!
HE'S BLUFFING.
OK, I'LL SEE YOUR 1000. WHAT'VE YOU GOT?
NOTHING.
PAIR OF JACKS.
DAMN YOUR EYES, WO-MAN!
SEE, I TOLD YOU HE WAS BLUFFING.
COME TO MOMMA.
AUDREY, IT'S YOUR DEAL.

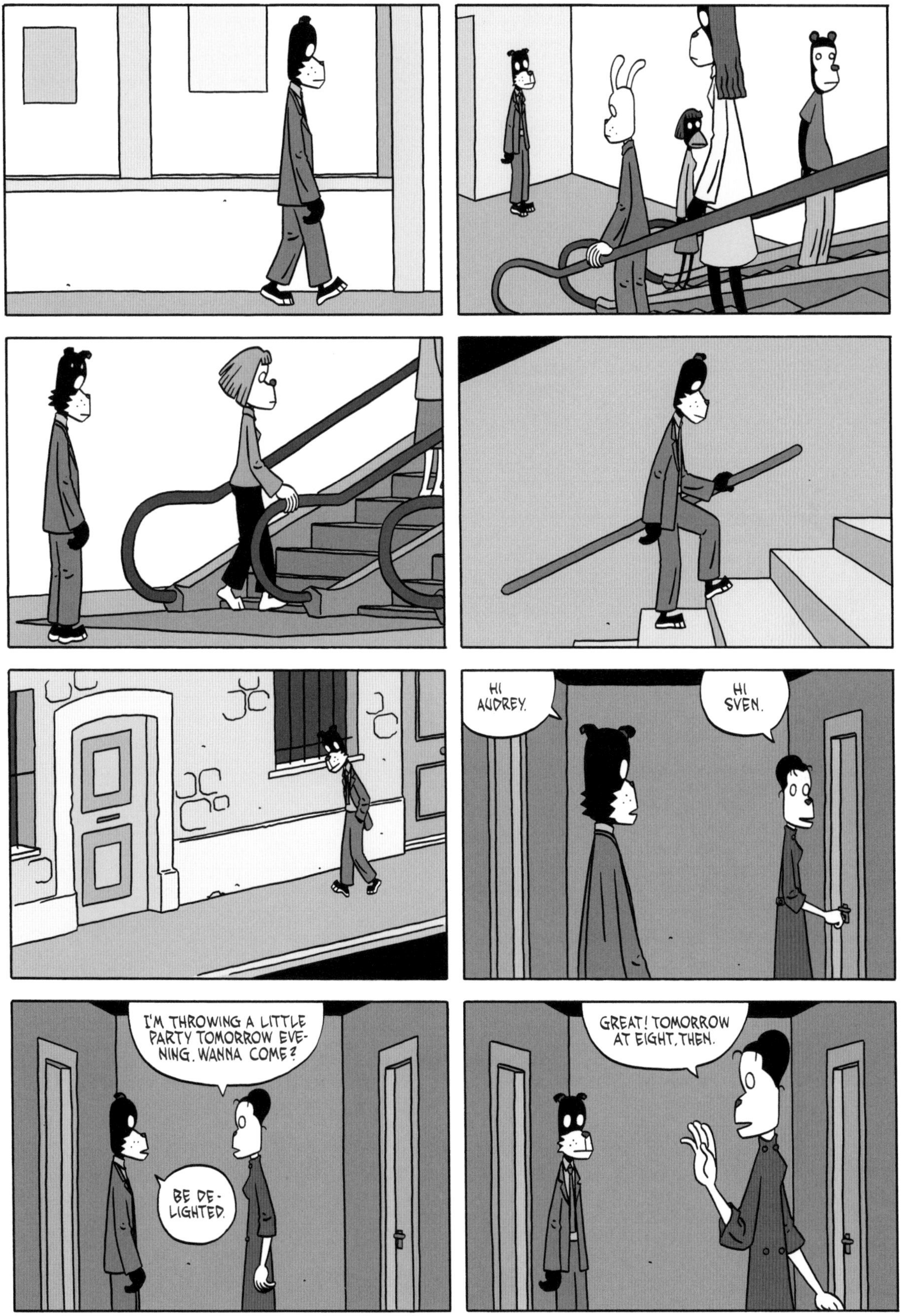
HI AUDREY.
HI SVEN.
I'M THROWING A LITTLE PARTY TOMORROW EVE- NING. WANNA COME?
BE DE- LIGHTED.
GREAT! TOMORROW AT EIGHT, THEN.

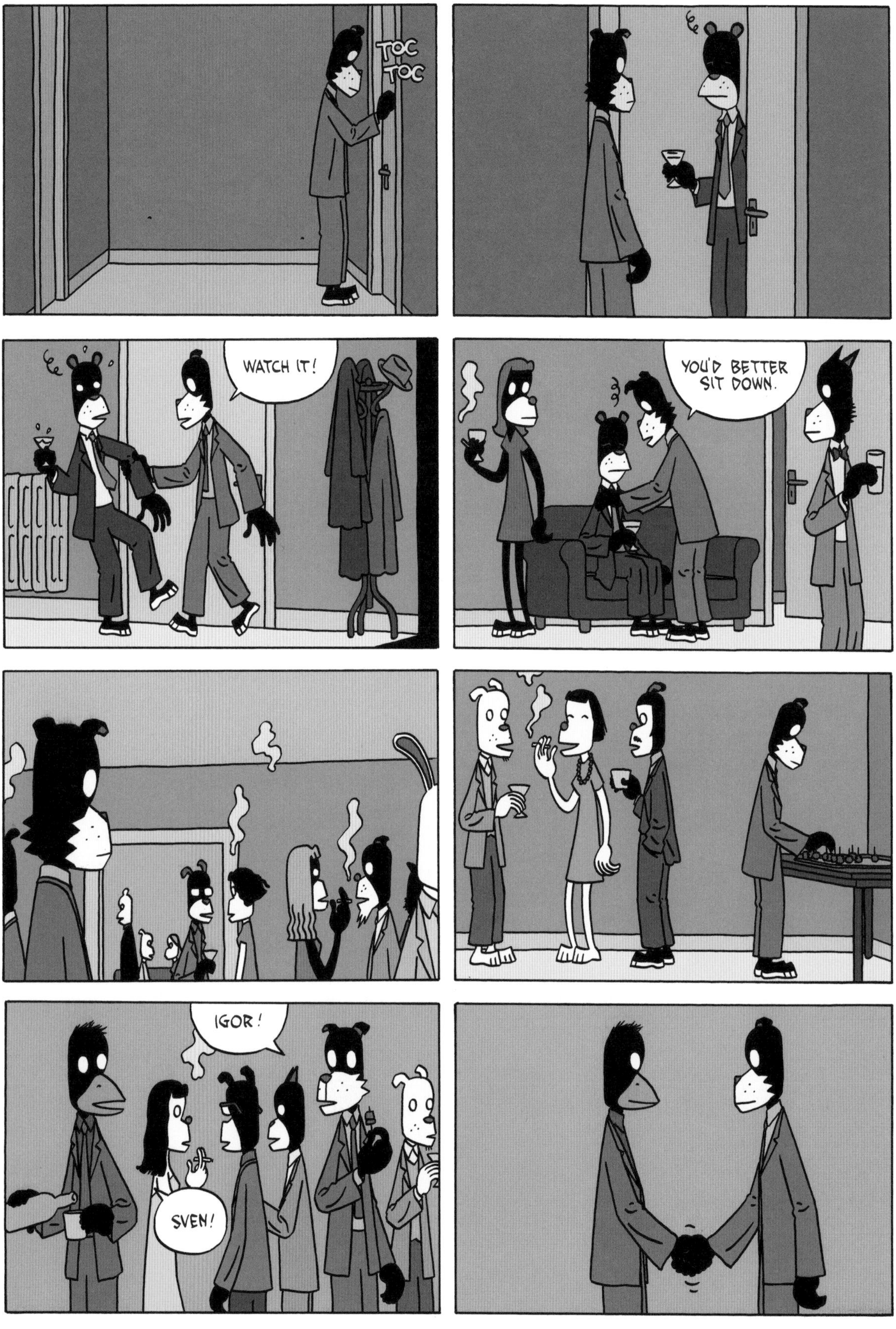
TOC TOC
WATCH IT!
YOU'D BETTER SIT DOWN.
IGOR!
SVEN!

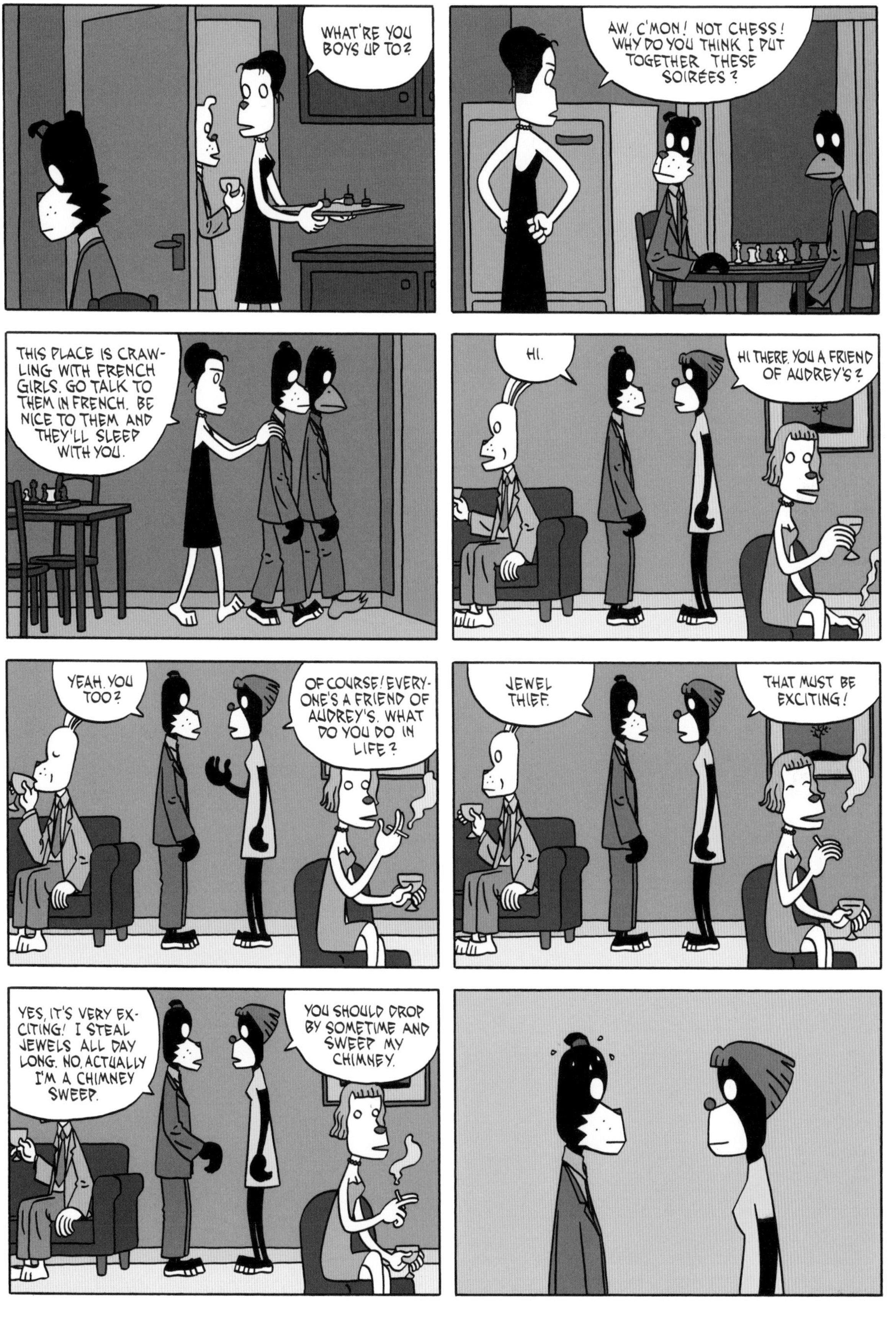
WHAT'RE YOU BOYS UP TO?
AW, C'MON! NOT CHESS! WHY DO YOU THINK I PUT TOGETHER THESE SOIRÉES?
THIS PLACE IS CRAWLING WITH FRENCH GIRLS. GO TALK TO THEM IN FRENCH. BE NICE TO THEM AND THEY'LL SLEEP WITH YOU.
HI.
HI THERE. YOU A FRIEND OF AUDREY'S?
YEAH. YOU TOO?
OF COURSE! EVERYONE'S A FRIEND OF AUDREY'S. WHAT DO YOU DO IN LIFE?
JEWEL THIEF.
THAT MUST BE EXCITING!
YES, IT'S VERY EXCITING! I STEAL JEWELS ALL DAY LONG. NO, ACTUALLY I'M A CHIMNEY SWEEP.
YOU SHOULD DROP BY SOMETIME AND SWEEP MY CHIMNEY.

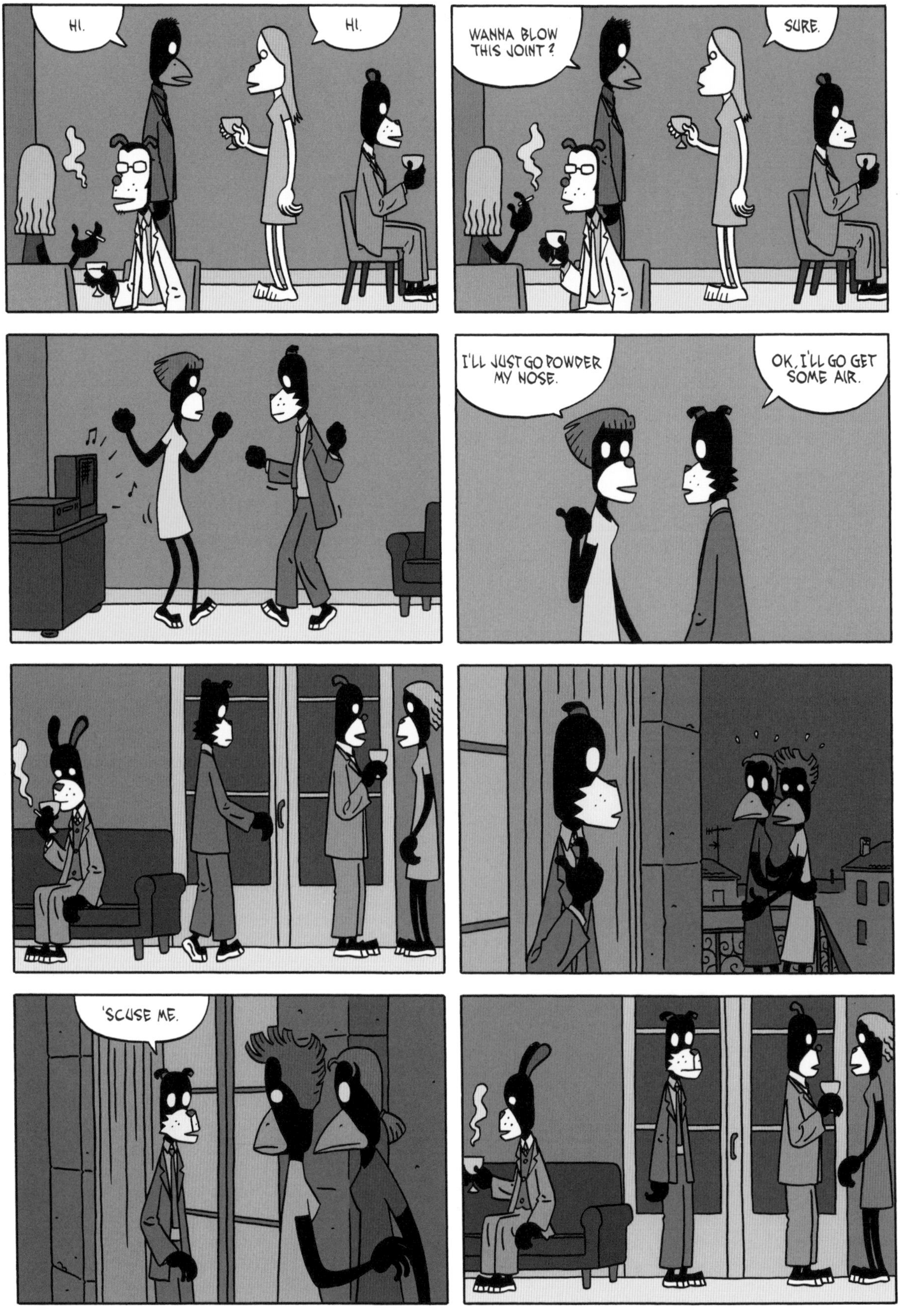
HI.
HI.
WANNA BLOW THIS JOINT?
SURE.
I'LL JUST GO POWDER MY NOSE.
OK, I'LL GO GET SOME AIR.
'SCUSE ME.

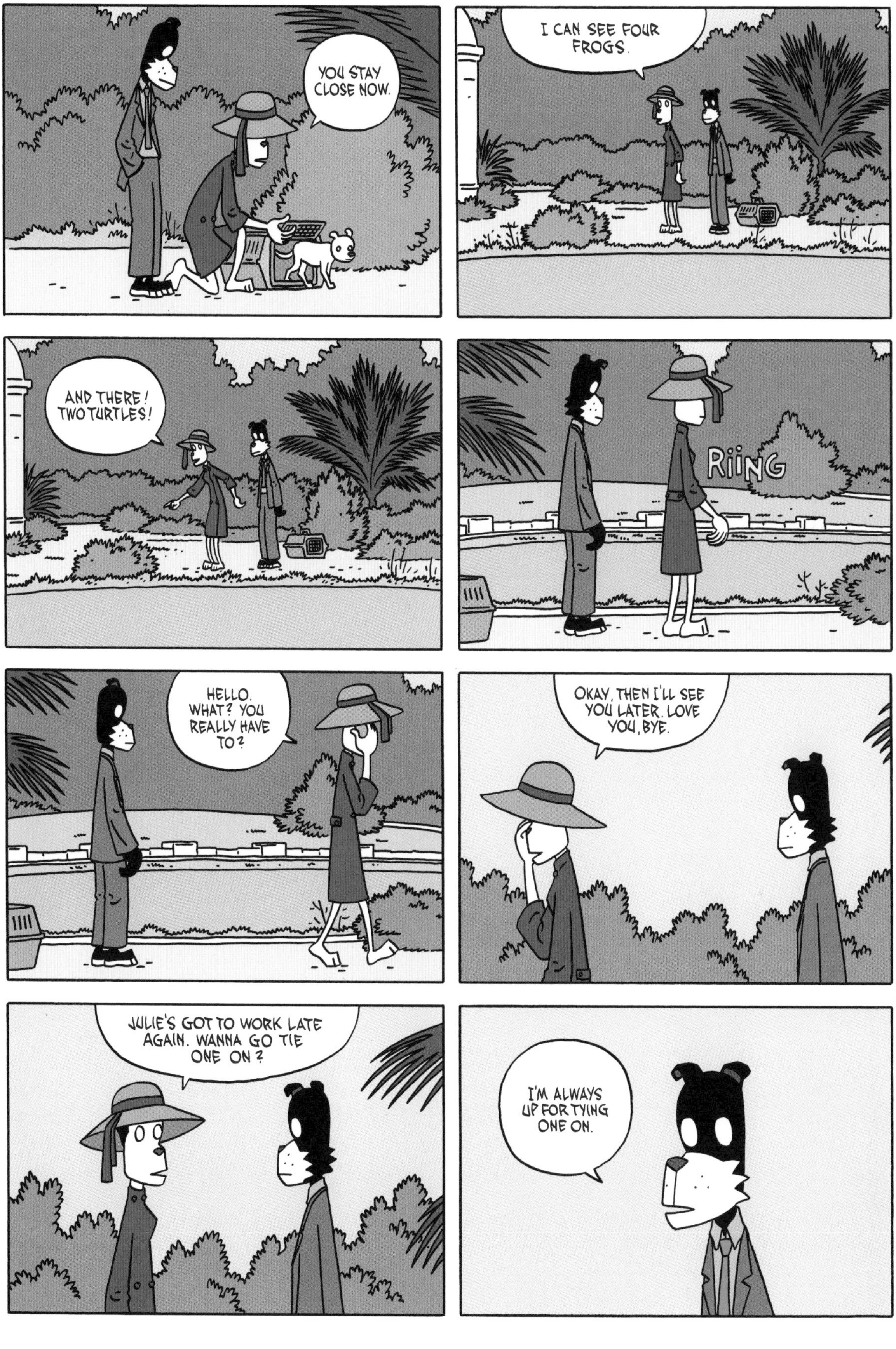
YOU STAY CLOSE NOW.
I CAN SEE FOUR FROGS.
AND THERE! TWO TURTLES!
RIING
HELLO. WHAT? YOU REALLY HAVE TO?
OKAY, THEN I'LL SEE YOU LATER. LOVE YOU, BYE.
JULIE'S GOT TO WORK LATE AGAIN. WANNA GO TIE ONE ON?
I'M ALWAYS UP FOR TYING ONE ON.

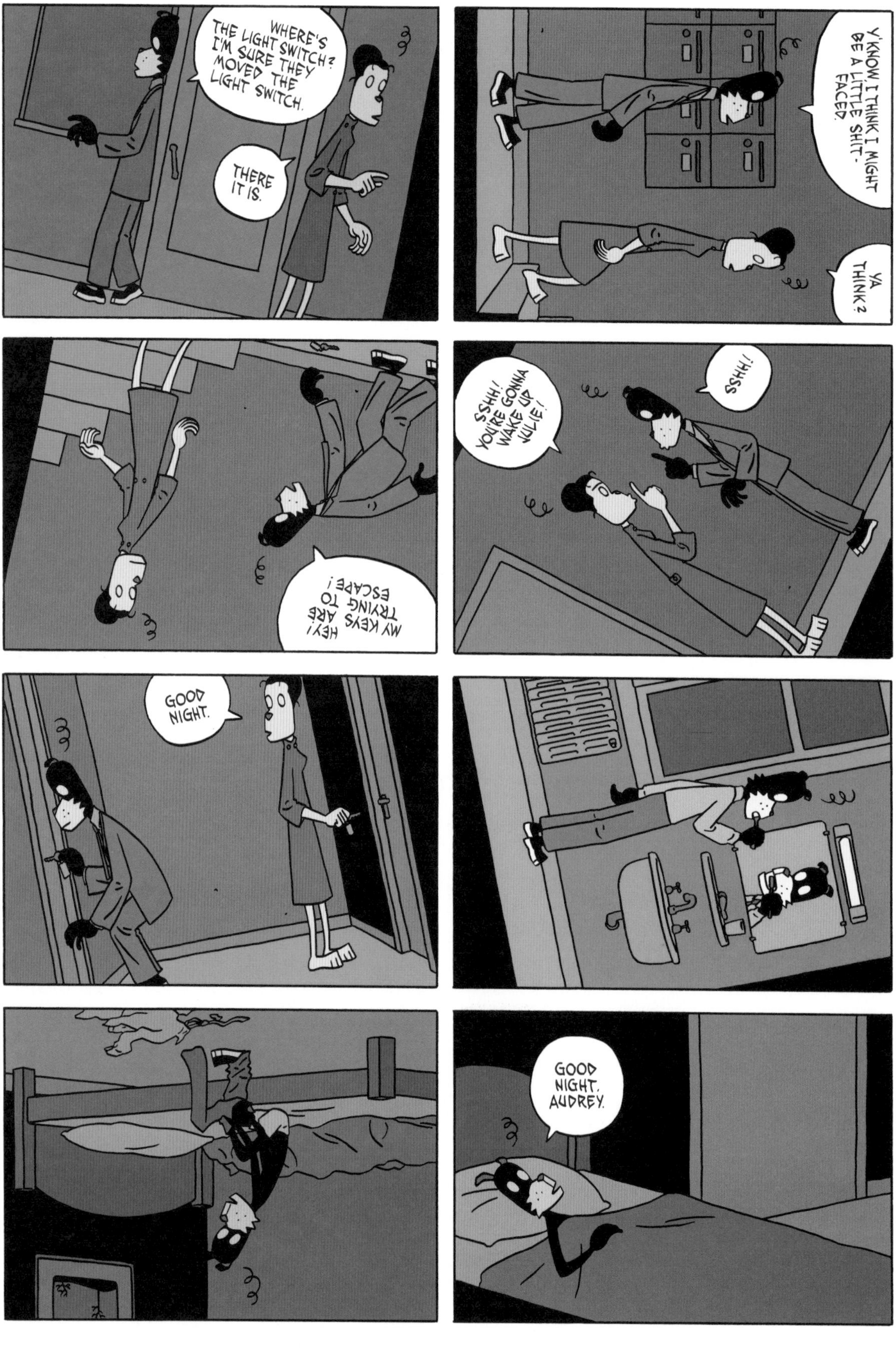
WHERE'S THE LIGHT SWITCH? I'M SURE THEY MOVED THE LIGHT SWITCH.
THERE IT IS.
Y'KNOW, I THINK I MIGHT BE A LITTLE SHIT-FACED.
YA THINK?
HEY! MY KEYS ARE TRYING TO ESCAPE!
SSHH! YOU'RE GONNA WAKE UP JULIE!
SSHH!
GOOD NIGHT.
GOOD NIGHT, AUDREY.

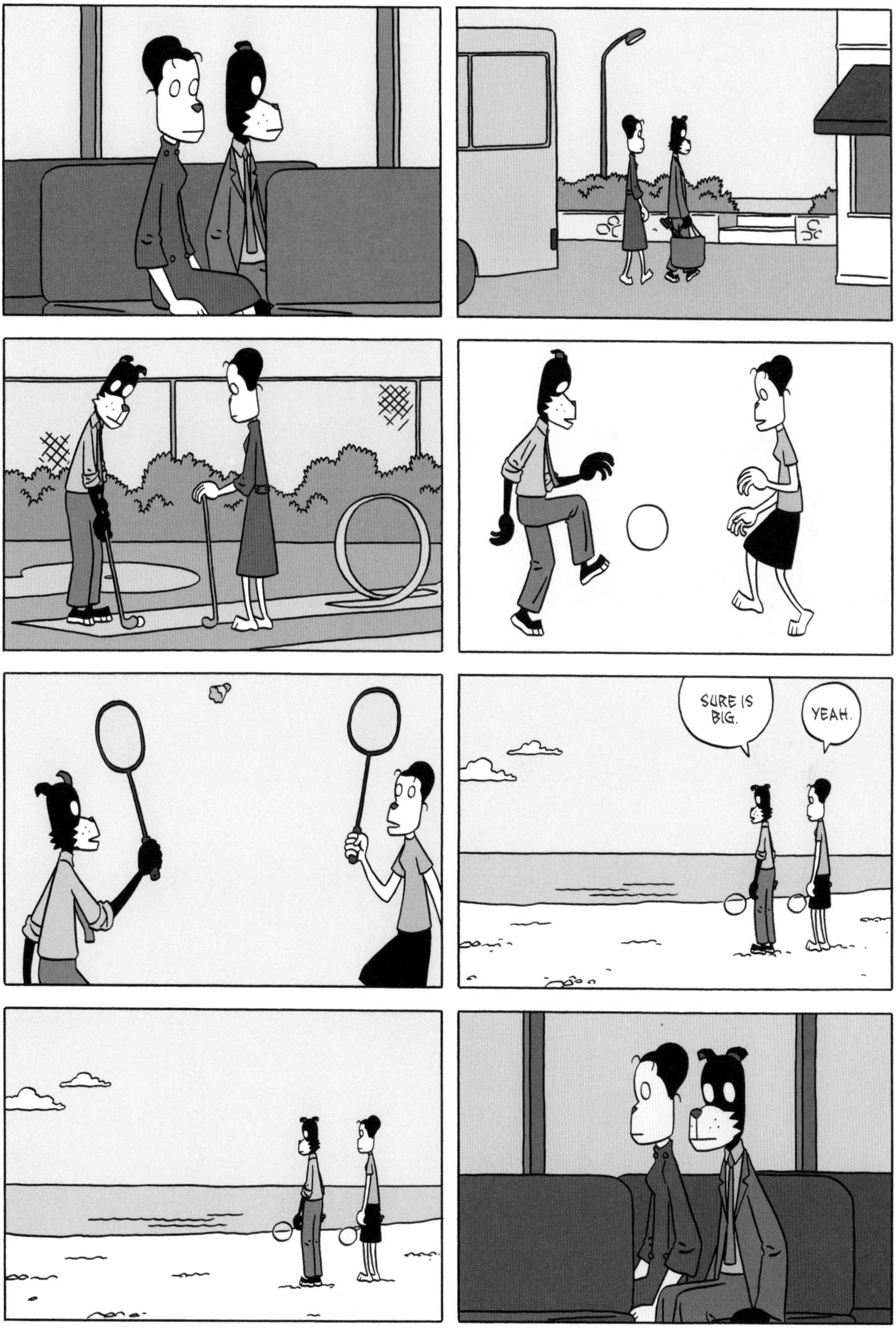
SURE IS BIG.
YEAH.

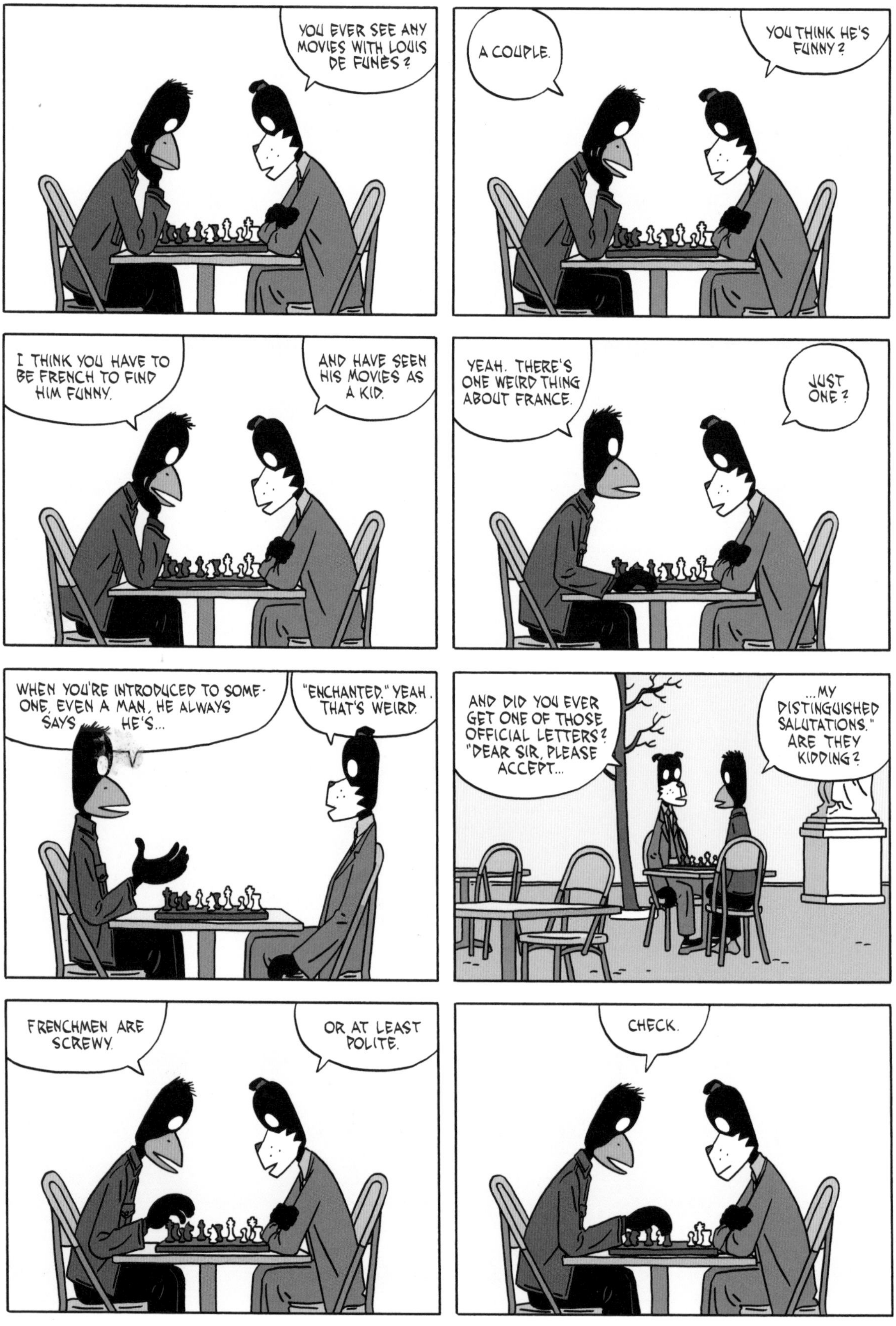
YOU EVER SEE ANY MOVIES WITH LOUIS DE FUNÈS?
A COUPLE.
YOU THINK HE'S FUNNY?
I THINK YOU HAVE TO BE FRENCH TO FIND HIM FUNNY.
AND HAVE SEEN HIS MOVIES AS A KID.
YEAH. THERE'S ONE WEIRD THING ABOUT FRANCE.
JUST ONE?
WHEN YOU'RE INTRODUCED TO SOMEONE, EVEN A MAN, HE ALWAYS SAYS HE'S...
"ENCHANTED." YEAH. THAT'S WEIRD.
AND DID YOU EVER GET ONE OF THOSE OFFICIAL LETTERS? "DEAR SIR, PLEASE ACCEPT...
...MY DISTINGUISHED SALUTATIONS." ARE THEY KIDDING?
FRENCHMEN ARE SCREWY.
OR AT LEAST POLITE.
CHECK.

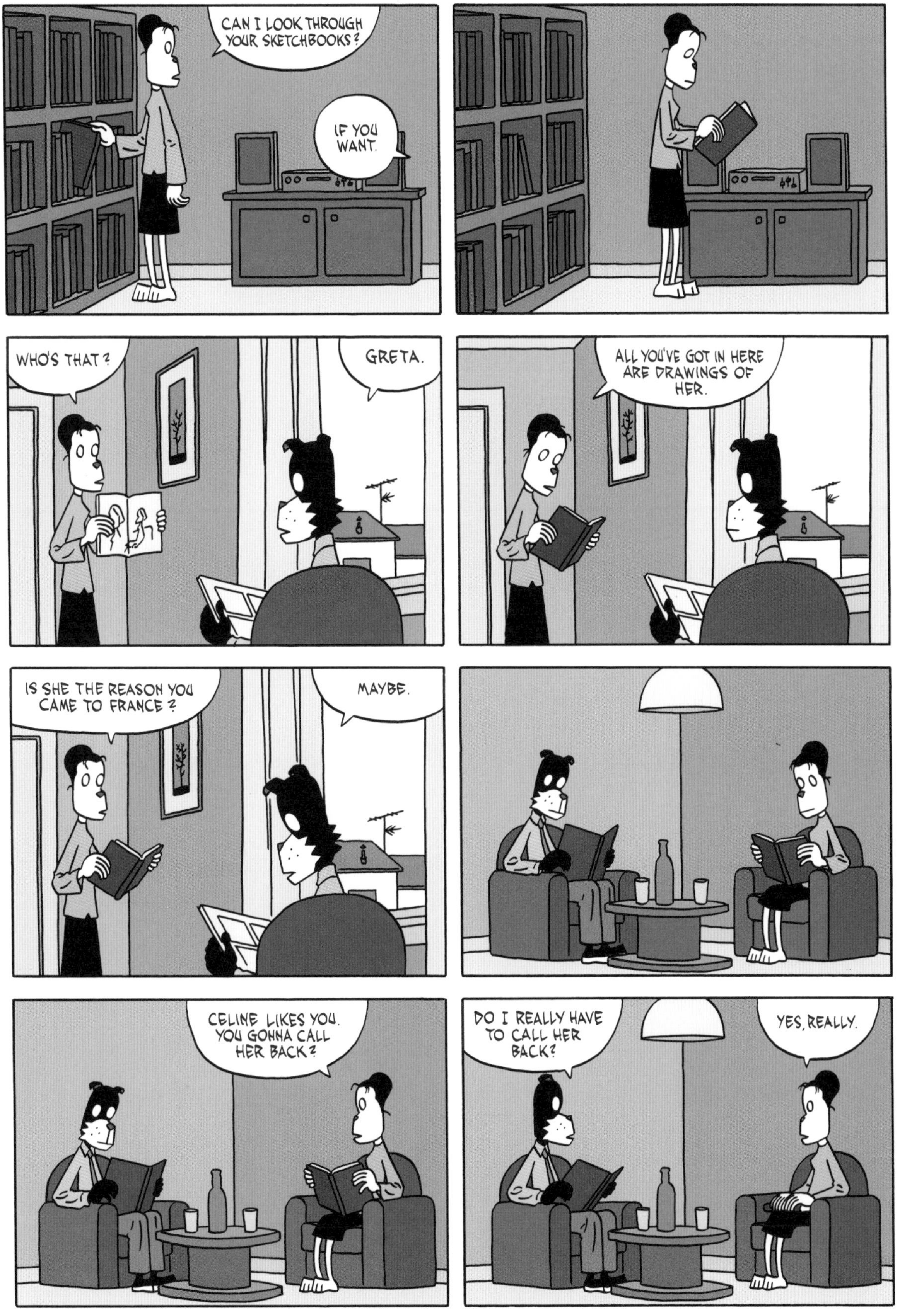
CAN I LOOK THROUGH YOUR SKETCHBOOKS?
IF YOU WANT.
WHO'S THAT?
GRETA.
ALL YOU'VE GOT IN HERE ARE DRAWINGS OF HER.
IS SHE THE REASON YOU CAME TO FRANCE?
MAYBE.
CELINE LIKES YOU. YOU GONNA CALL HER BACK?
DO I REALLY HAVE TO CALL HER BACK?
YES, REALLY.

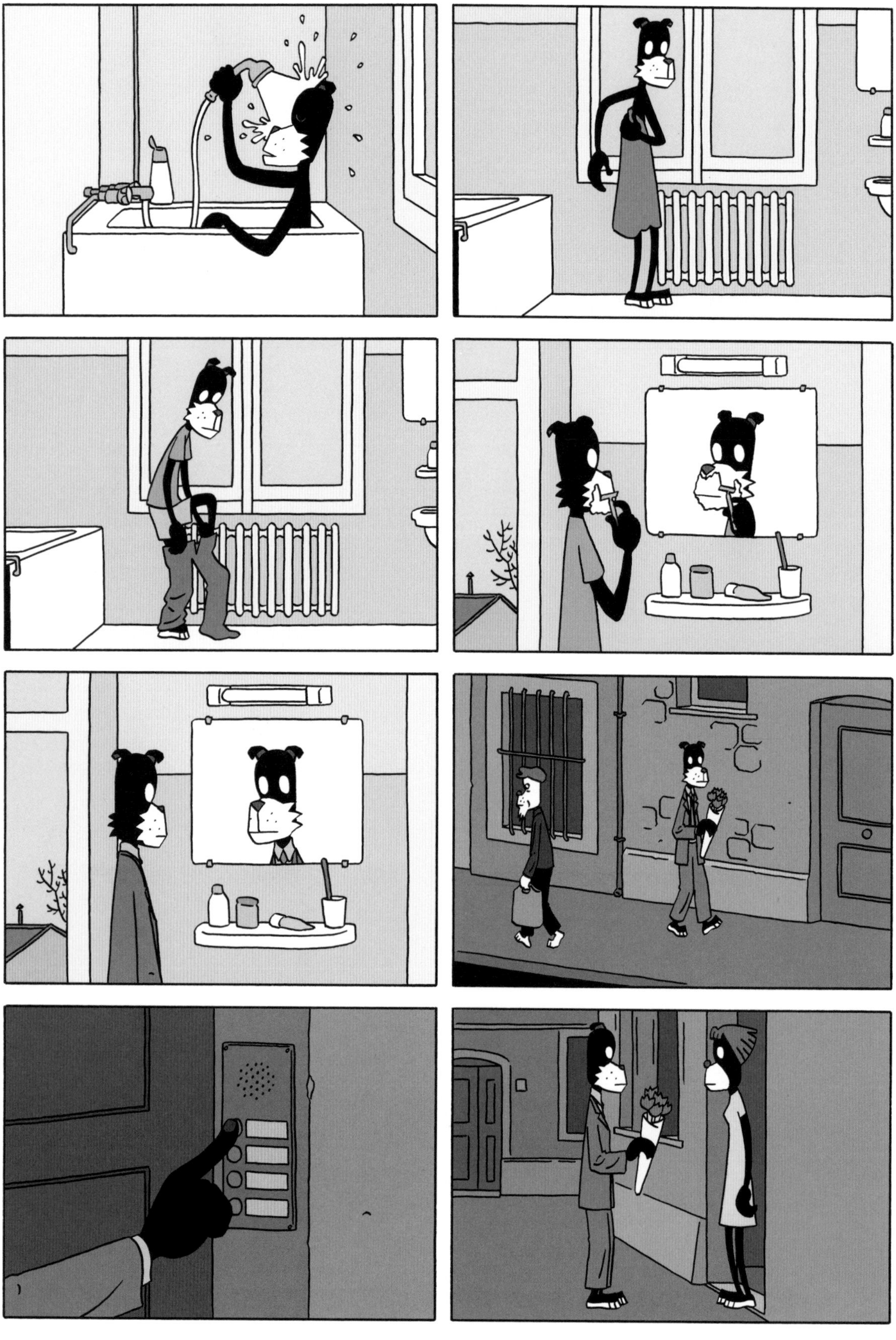

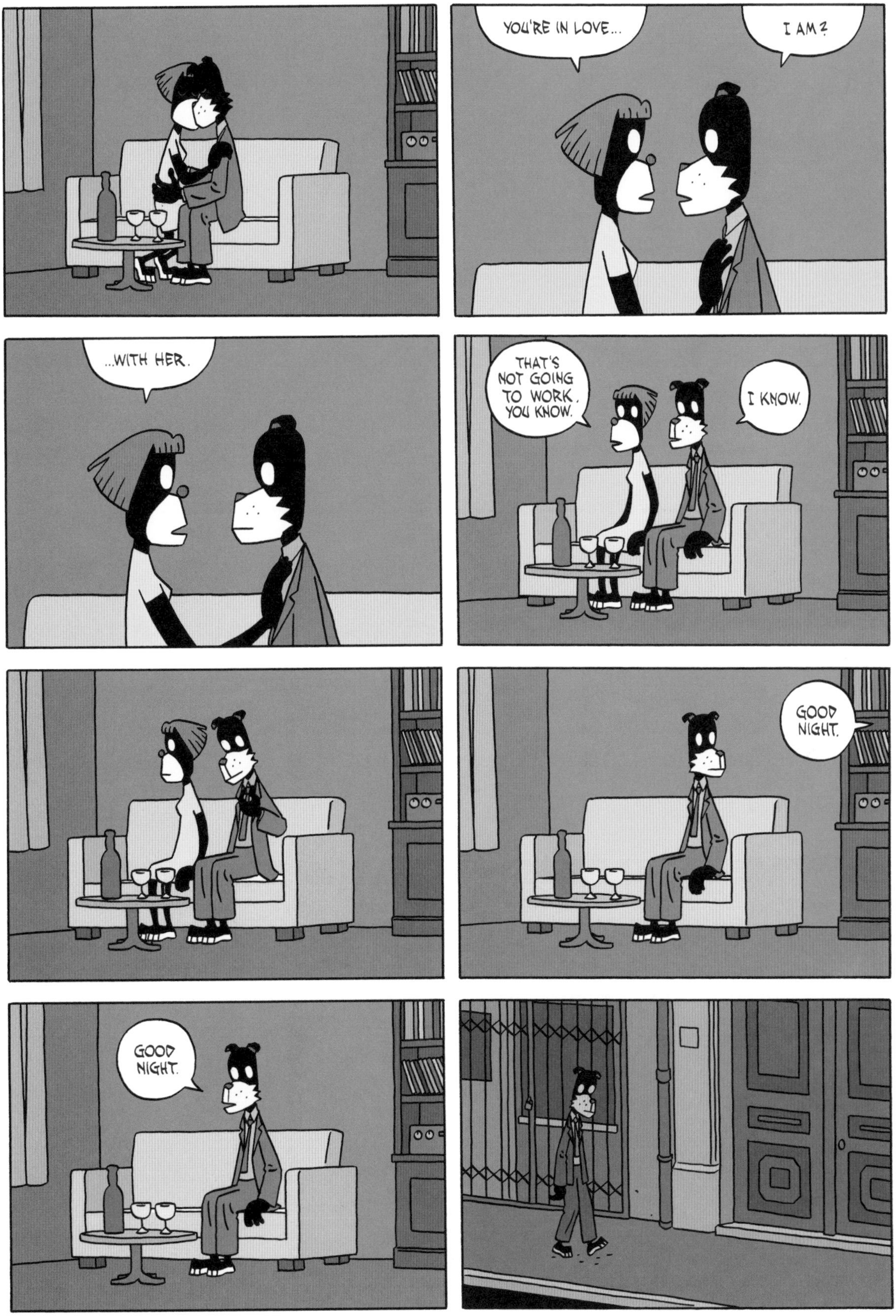
YOU'RE IN LOVE...
I AM?
...WITH HER.
THAT'S NOT GOING TO WORK, YOU KNOW.
I KNOW.
GOOD NIGHT.
GOOD NIGHT.

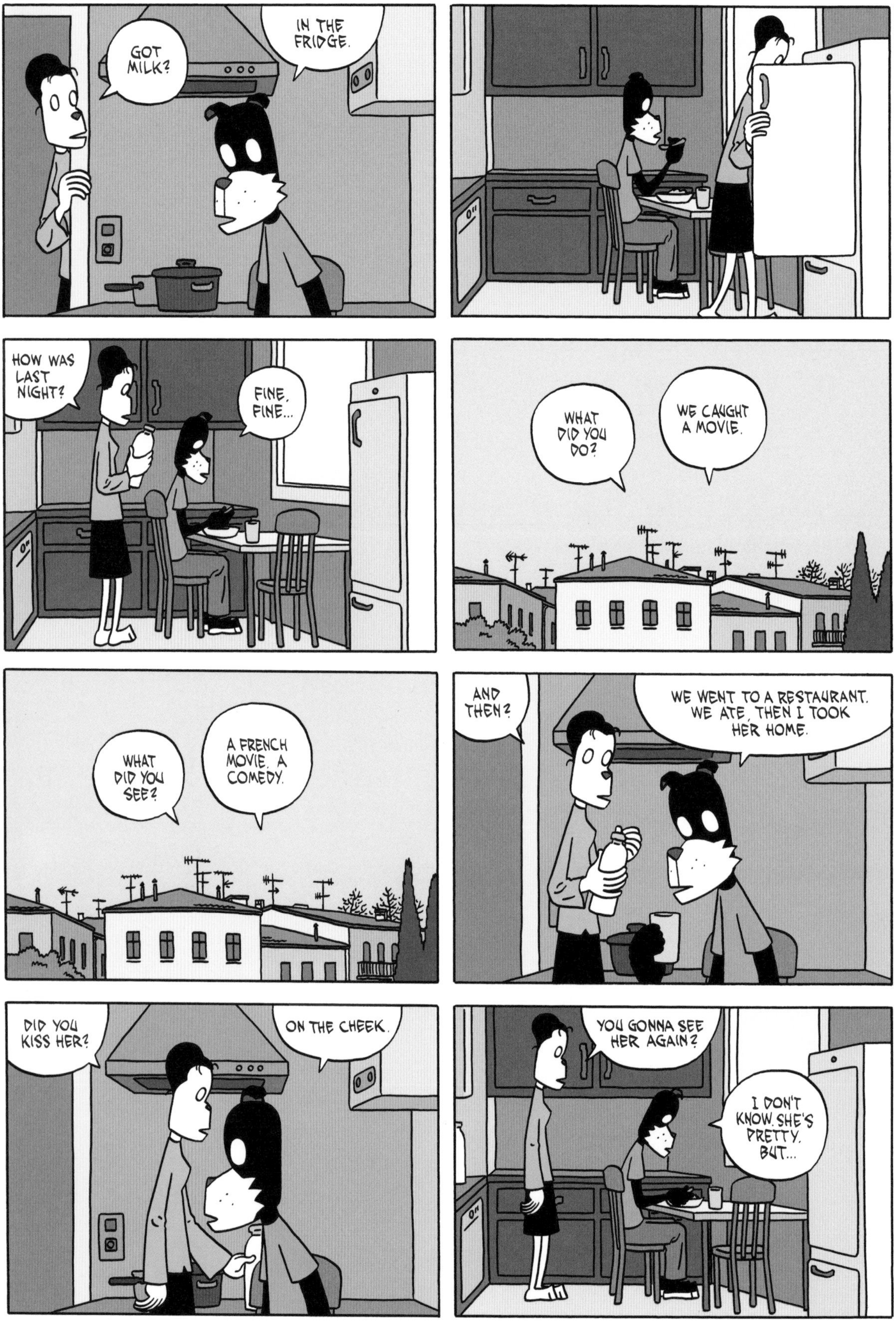
GOT MILK?
IN THE FRIDGE.
HOW WAS LAST NIGHT?
FINE, FINE...
WHAT DID YOU DO?
WE CAUGHT A MOVIE.
WHAT DID YOU SEE?
A FRENCH MOVIE. A COMEDY.
AND THEN?
WE WENT TO A RESTAURANT. WE ATE, THEN I TOOK HER HOME.
DID YOU KISS HER?
ON THE CHEEK.
YOU GONNA SEE HER AGAIN?
I DON'T KNOW. SHE'S PRETTY, BUT...

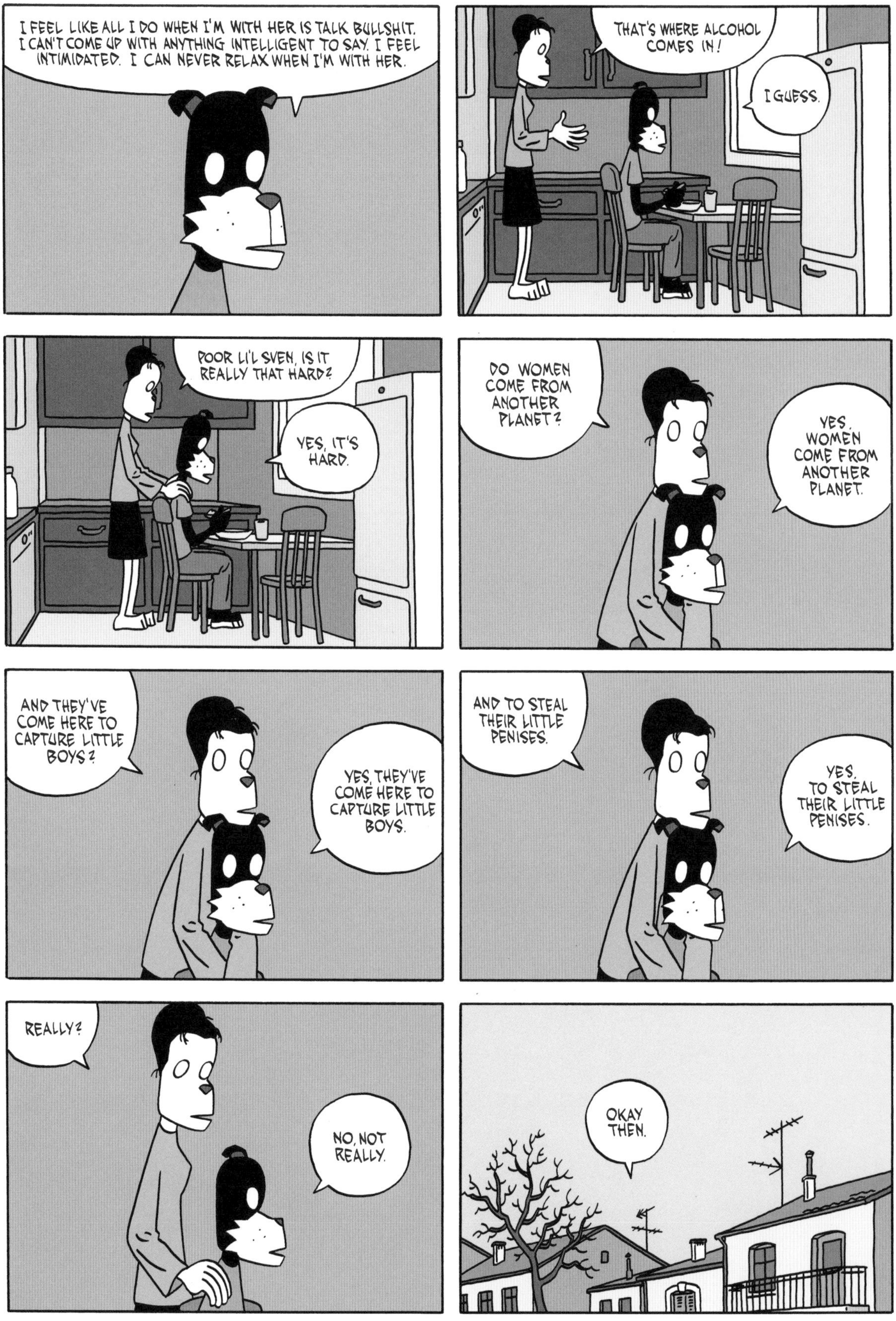
I FEEL LIKE ALL I DO WHEN I'M WITH HER IS TALK BULLSHIT. I CAN'T COME UP WITH ANYTHING INTELLIGENT TO SAY. I FEEL INTIMIDATED. I CAN NEVER RELAX WHEN I'M WITH HER.
THAT'S WHERE ALCOHOL COMES IN!
I GUESS.
POOR LI'L SVEN, IS IT REALLY THAT HARD?
YES, IT'S HARD.
DO WOMEN COME FROM ANOTHER PLANET?
YES. WOMEN COME FROM ANOTHER PLANET.
AND THEY'VE COME HERE TO CAPTURE LITTLE BOYS?
YES, THEY'VE COME HERE TO CAPTURE LITTLE BOYS.
AND TO STEAL THEIR LITTLE PENISES.
YES. TO STEAL THEIR LITTLE PENISES.
REALLY?
NO, NOT REALLY.
OKAY THEN.

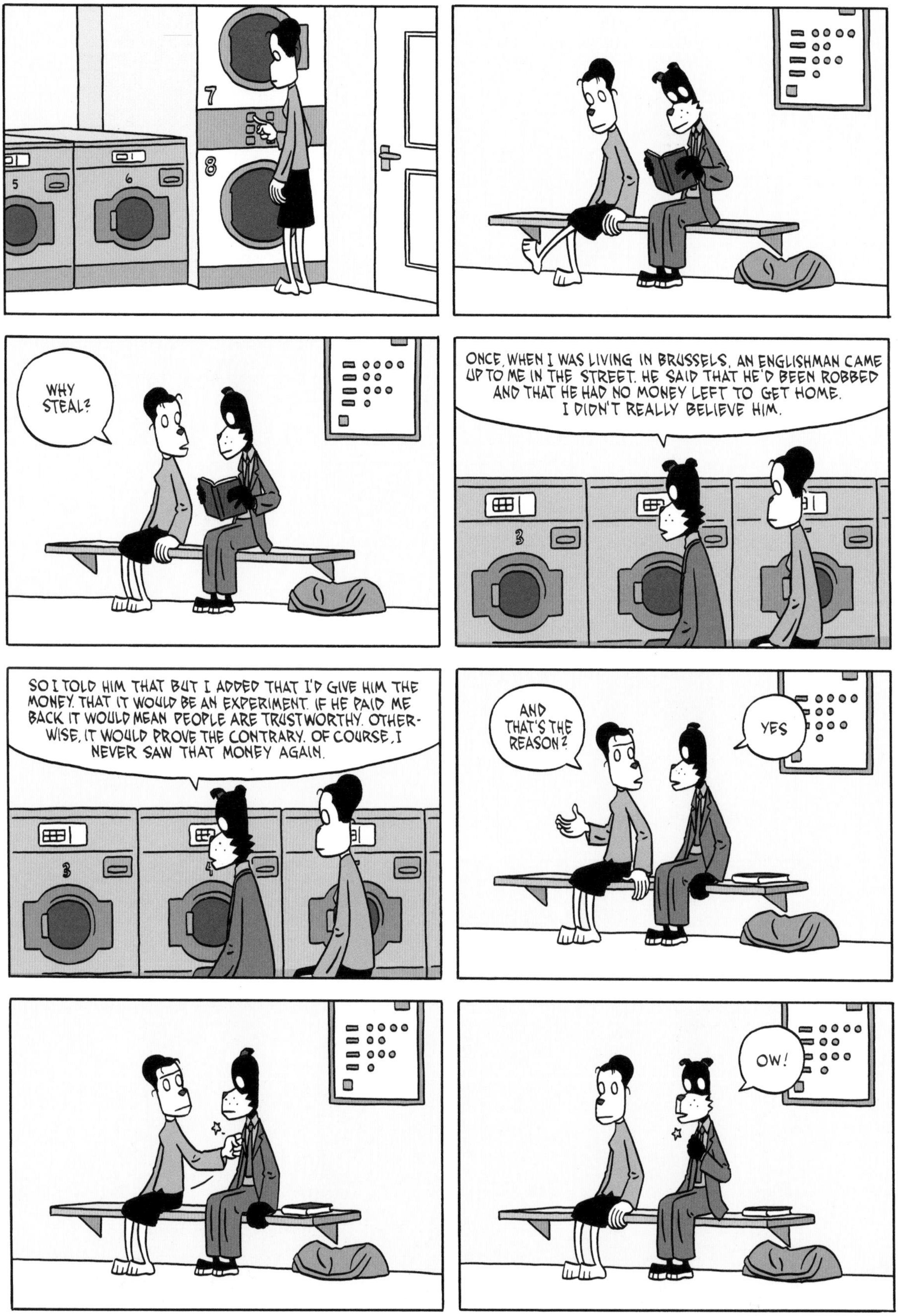
WHY STEAL?
ONCE, WHEN I WAS LIVING IN BRUSSELS, AN ENGLISHMAN CAME UP TO ME IN THE STREET. HE SAID THAT HE'D BEEN ROBBED AND THAT HE HAD NO MONEY LEFT TO GET HOME. I DIDN'T REALLY BELIEVE HIM.
SO I TOLD HIM THAT BUT I ADDED THAT I'D GIVE HIM THE MONEY. THAT IT WOULD BE AN EXPERIMENT. IF HE PAID ME BACK IT WOULD MEAN PEOPLE ARE TRUSTWORTHY. OTHERWISE, IT WOULD PROVE THE CONTRARY. OF COURSE, I NEVER SAW THAT MONEY AGAIN.
AND THAT'S THE REASON?
YES
OW!

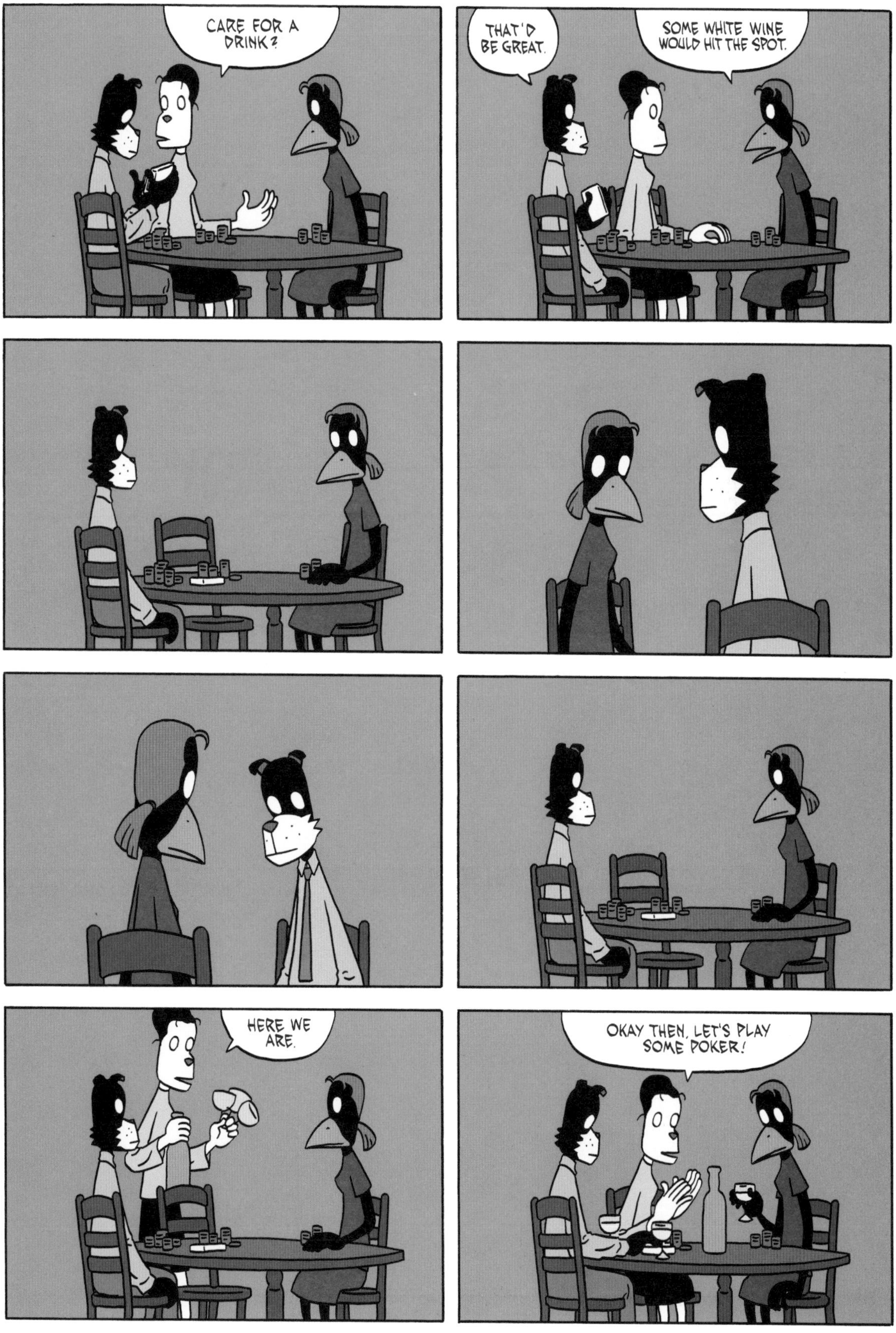
CARE FOR A DRINK?
THAT'D BE GREAT.
SOME WHITE WINE WOULD HIT THE SPOT.
HERE WE ARE.
OKAY THEN, LET'S PLAY SOME POKER!

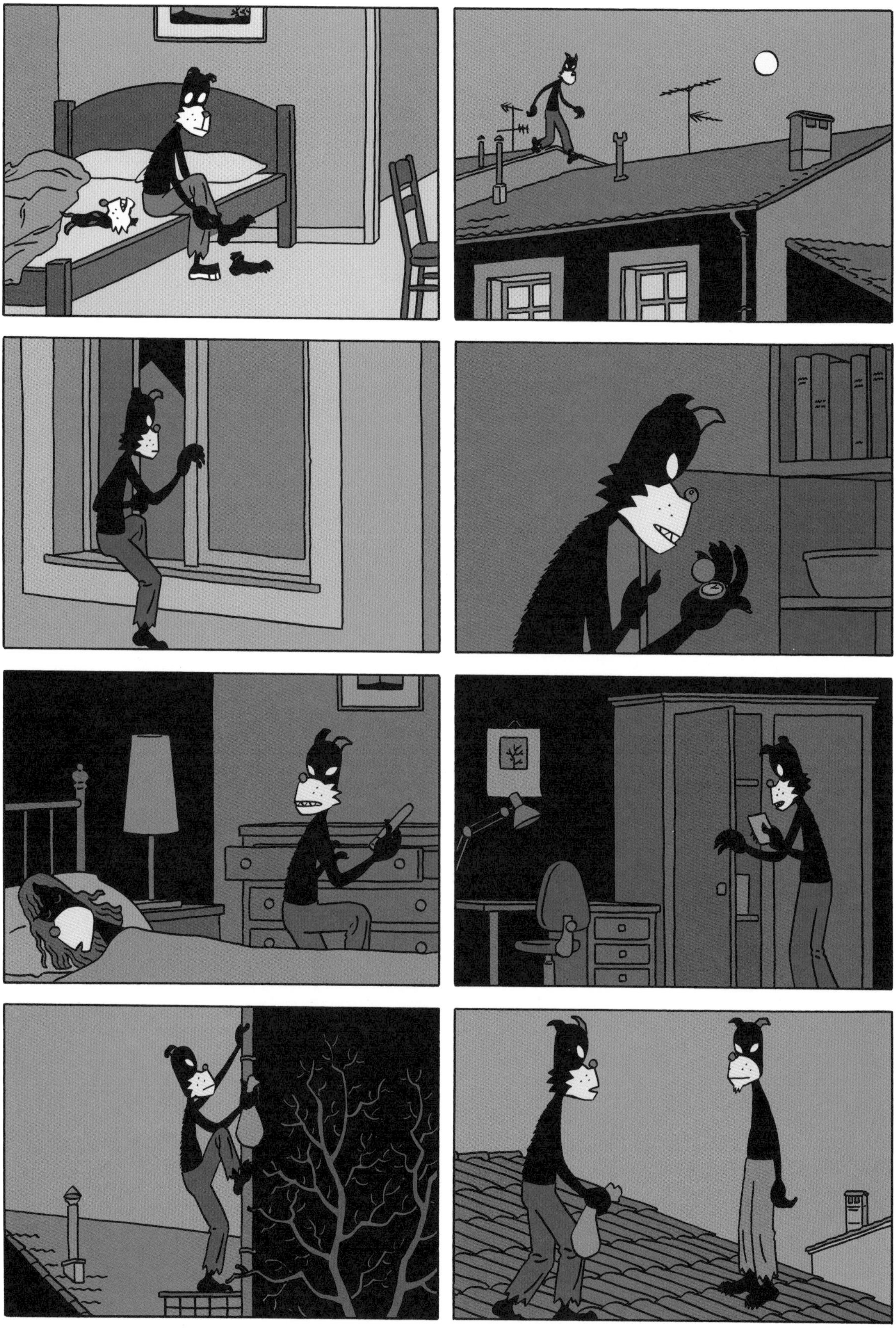

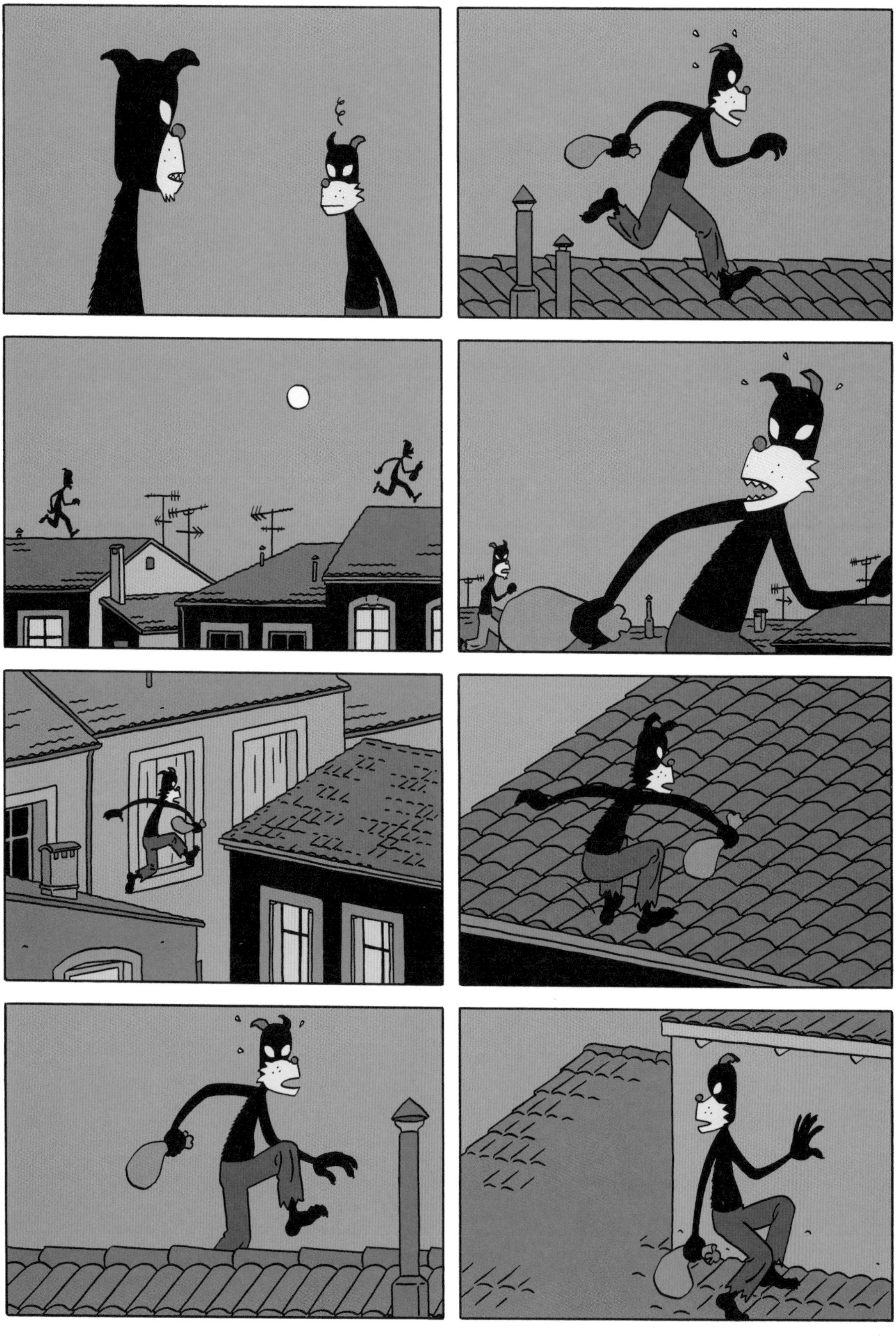

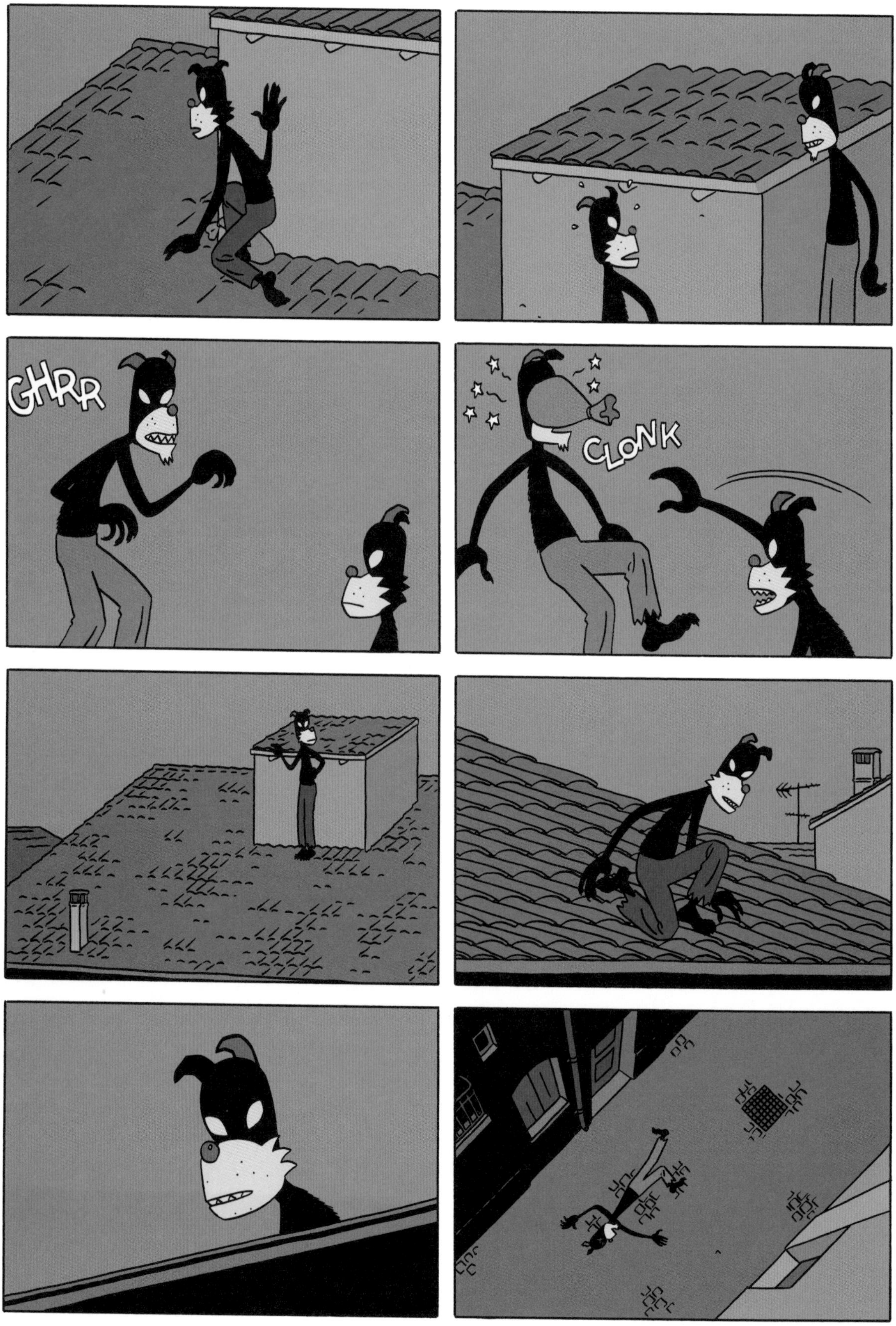
GHRR
CLONK

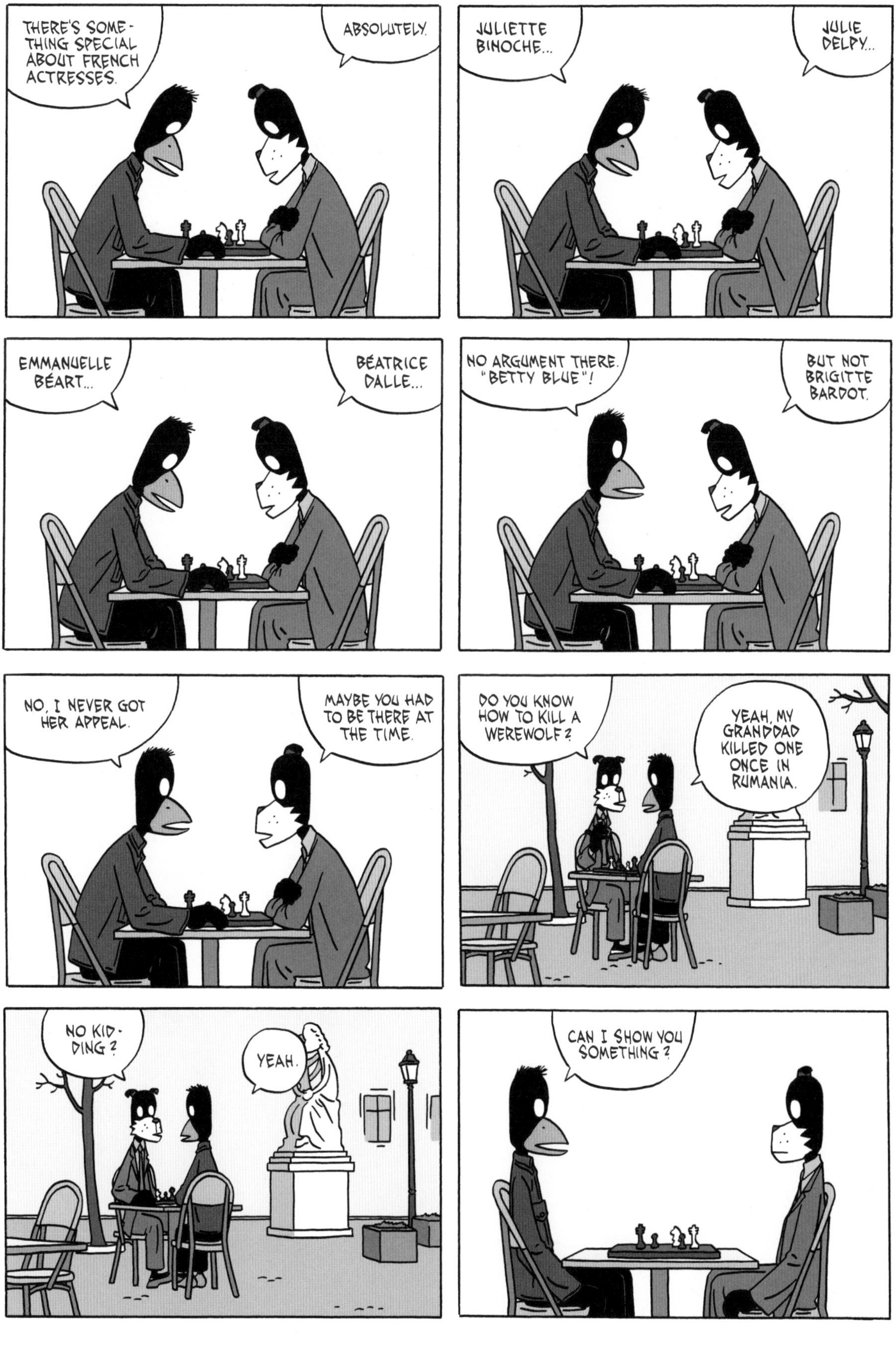
THERE'S SOMETHING SPECIAL ABOUT FRENCH ACTRESSES.
ABSOLUTELY.
JULIETTE BINOCHE...
JULIE DELPY...
EMMANUELLE BÉART...
BÉATRICE DALLE...
NO ARGUMENT THERE. "BETTY BLUE"!
BUT NOT BRIGITTE BARDOT.
NO, I NEVER GOT HER APPEAL.
MAYBE YOU HAD TO BE THERE AT THE TIME.
DO YOU KNOW HOW TO KILL A WEREWOLF?
YEAH, MY GRANDDAD KILLED ONE ONCE IN RUMANIA.
NO KIDDING?
YEAH.
CAN I SHOW YOU SOMETHING?

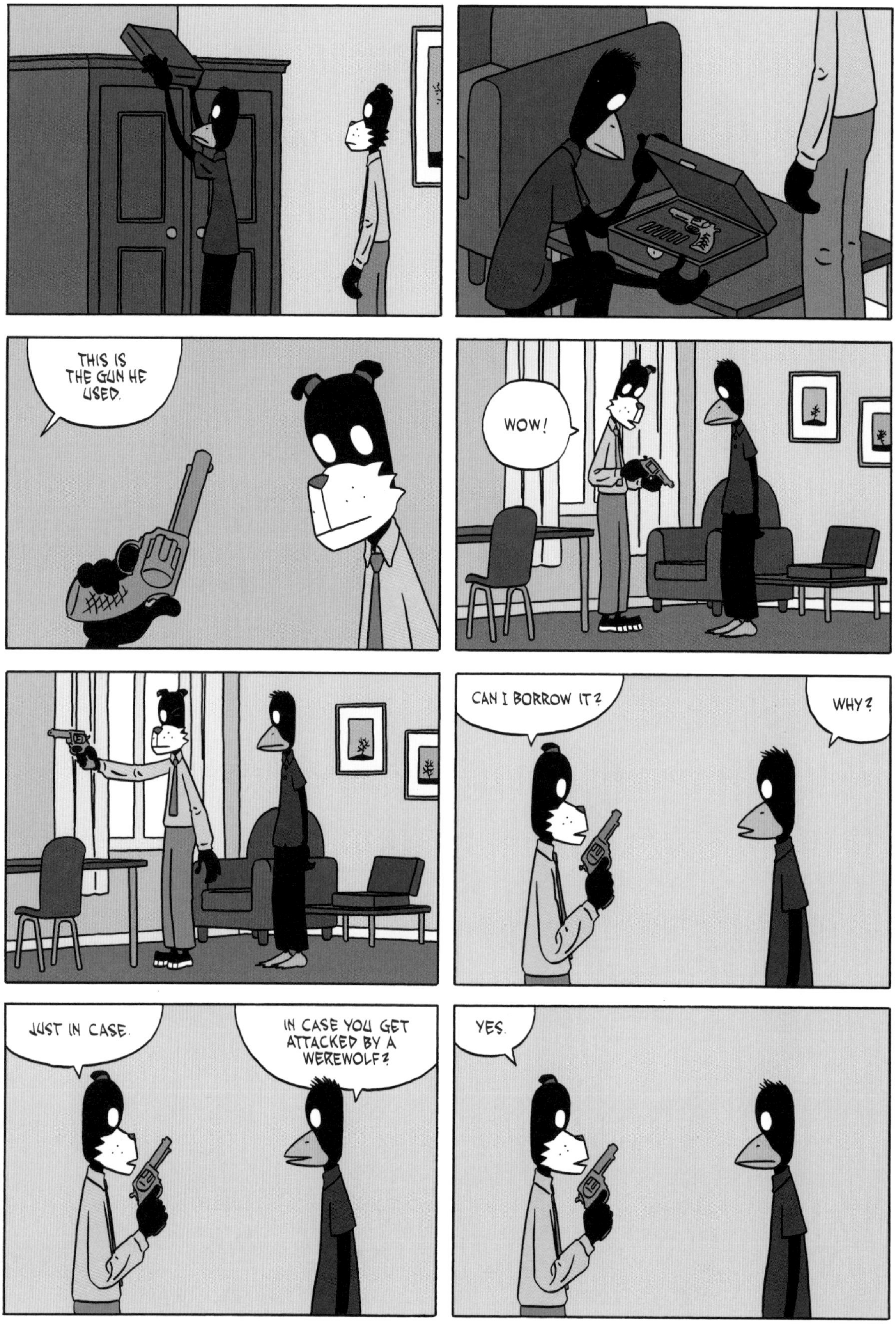
THIS IS THE GUN HE USED.
WOW!
CAN I BORROW IT?
WHY?
JUST IN CASE.
IN CASE YOU GET ATTACKED BY A WEREWOLF?
YES.

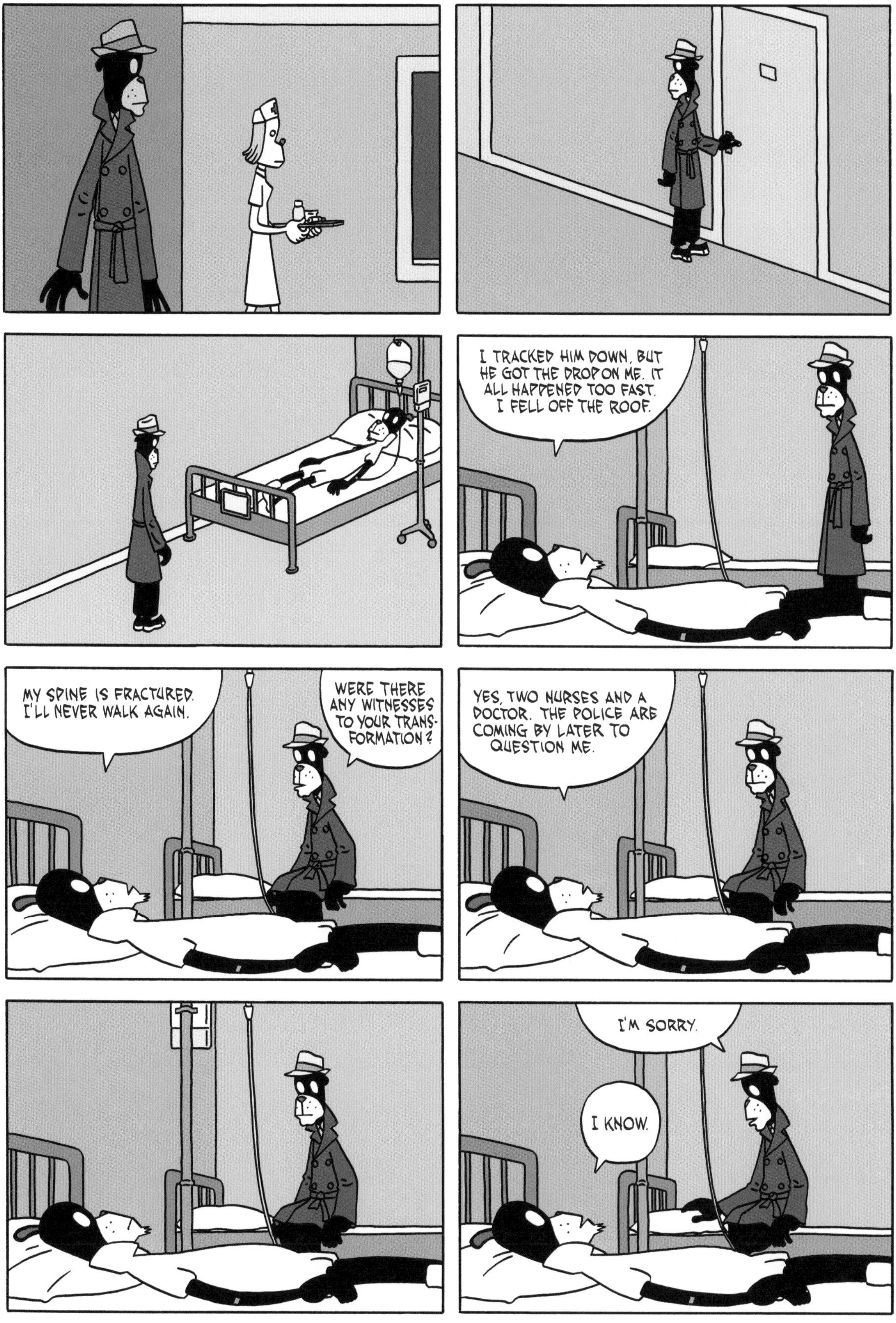
I TRACKED HIM DOWN, BUT HE GOT THE DROP ON ME. IT ALL HAPPENED TOO FAST. I FELL OFF THE ROOF.
MY SPINE IS FRACTURED. I'LL NEVER WALK AGAIN.
WERE THERE ANY WITNESSES TO YOUR TRANS-FORMATION?
YES, TWO NURSES AND A DOCTOR. THE POLICE ARE COMING BY LATER TO QUESTION ME.
I'M SORRY.
I KNOW.

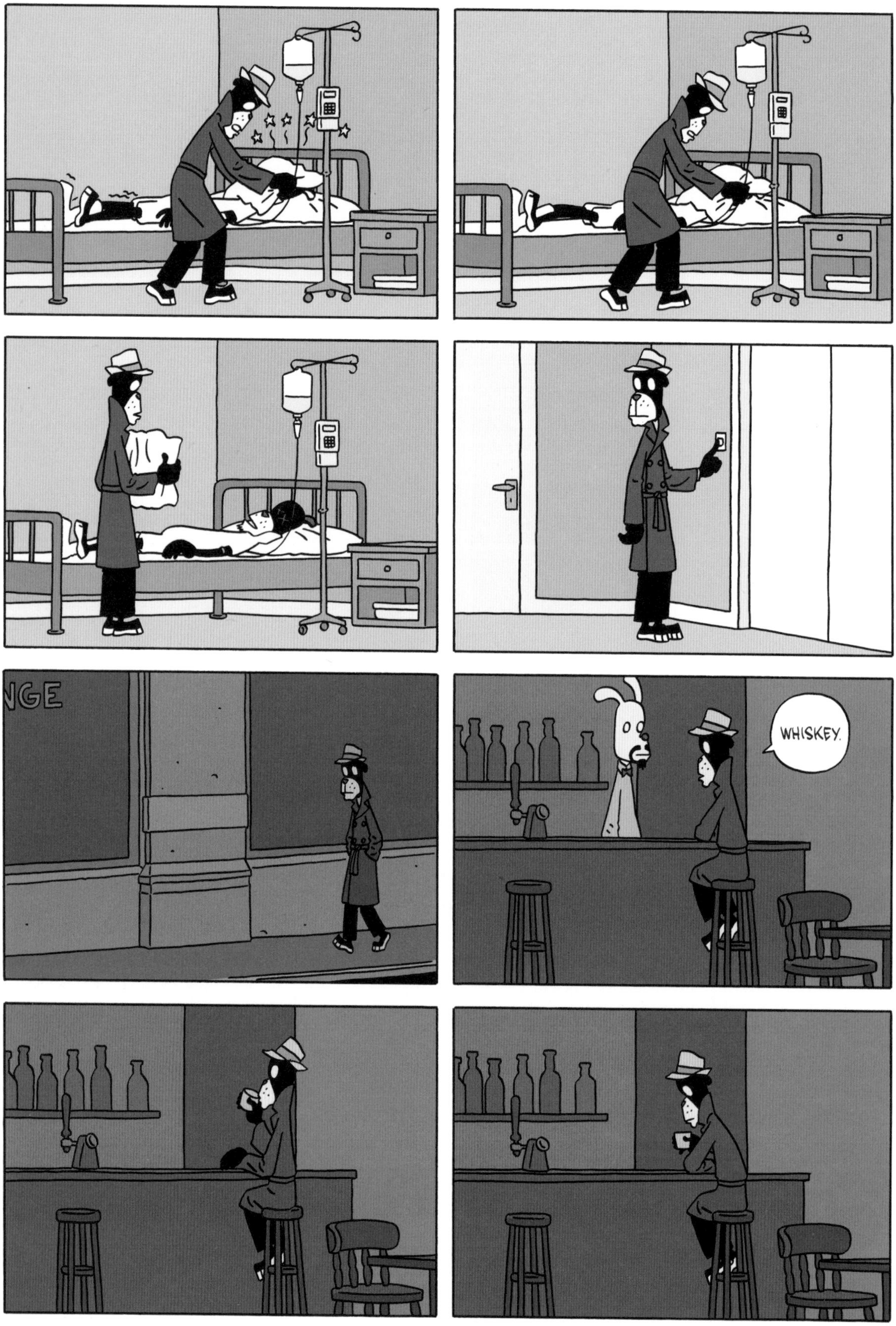
NGE
WHISKEY.

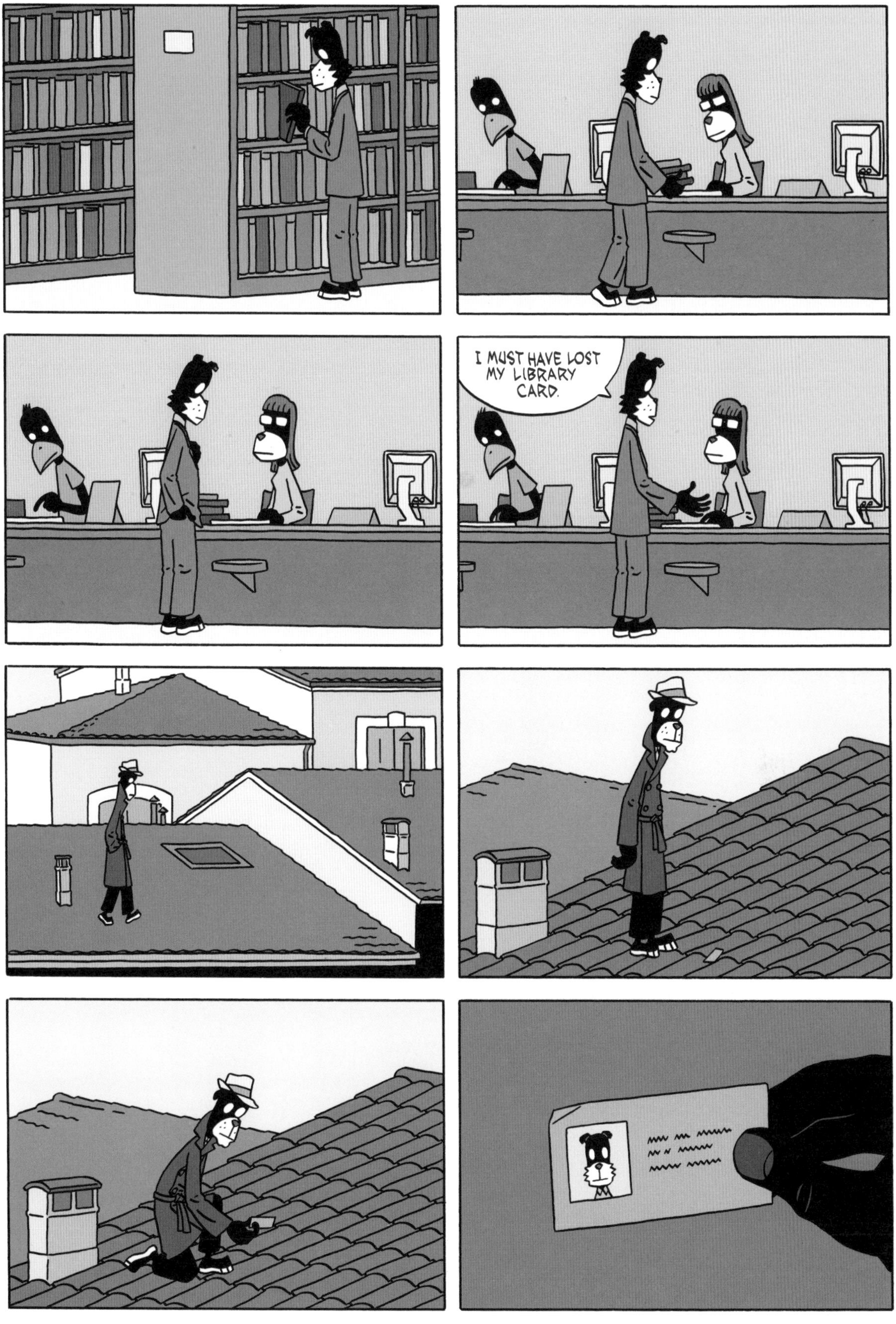
I MUST HAVE LOST MY LIBRARY CARD.

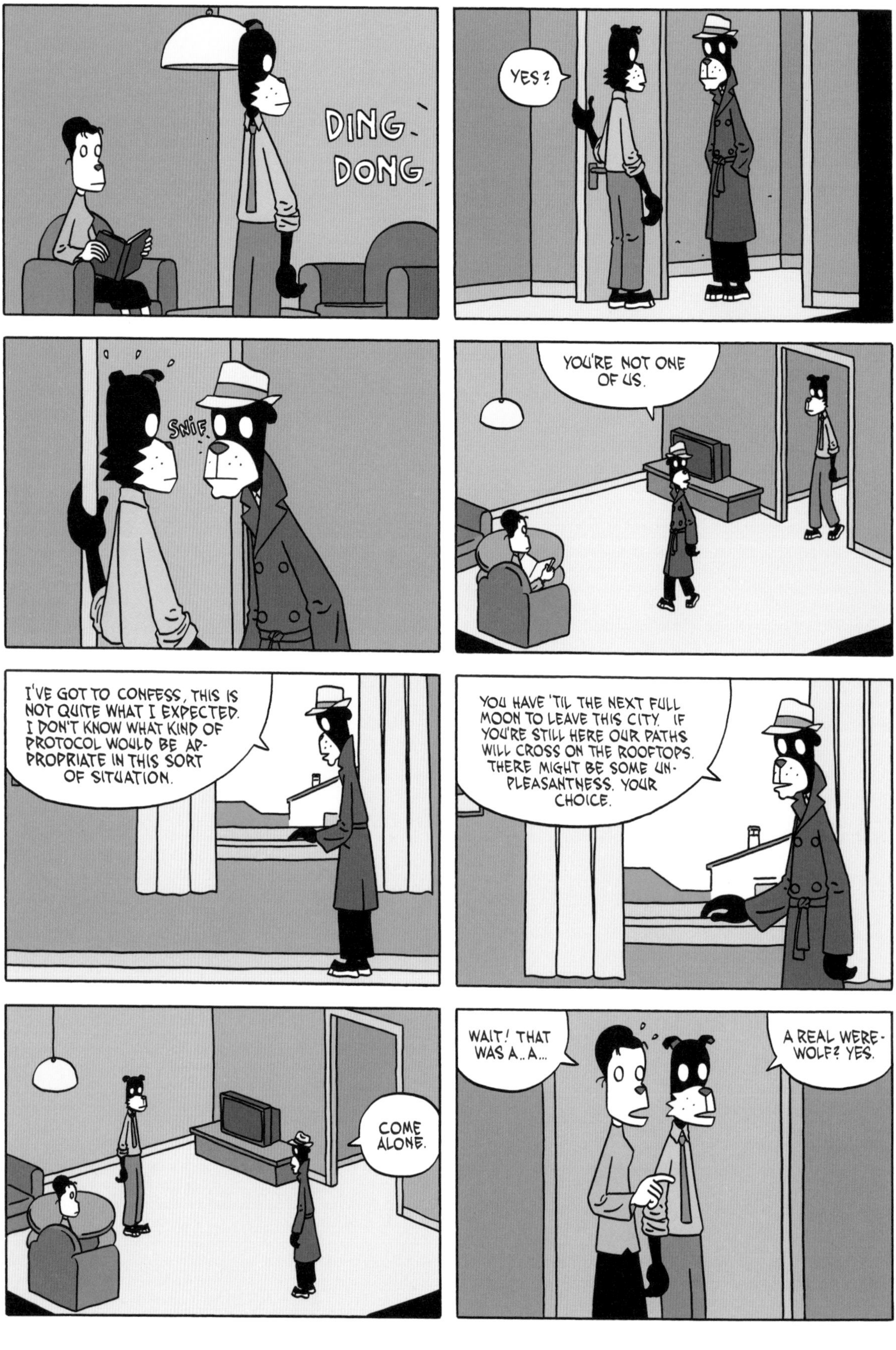
DING
DONG
YES?
SNIF
YOU'RE NOT ONE OF US.
I'VE GOT TO CONFESS, THIS IS NOT QUITE WHAT I EXPECTED. I DON'T KNOW WHAT KIND OF PROTOCOL WOULD BE AP-PROPRIATE IN THIS SORT OF SITUATION.
YOU HAVE 'TIL THE NEXT FULL MOON TO LEAVE THIS CITY. IF YOU'RE STILL HERE OUR PATHS WILL CROSS ON THE ROOFTOPS. THERE MIGHT BE SOME UN-PLEASANTNESS. YOUR CHOICE.
COME ALONE.
WAIT! THAT WAS A.. A...
A REAL WERE-WOLF? YES.

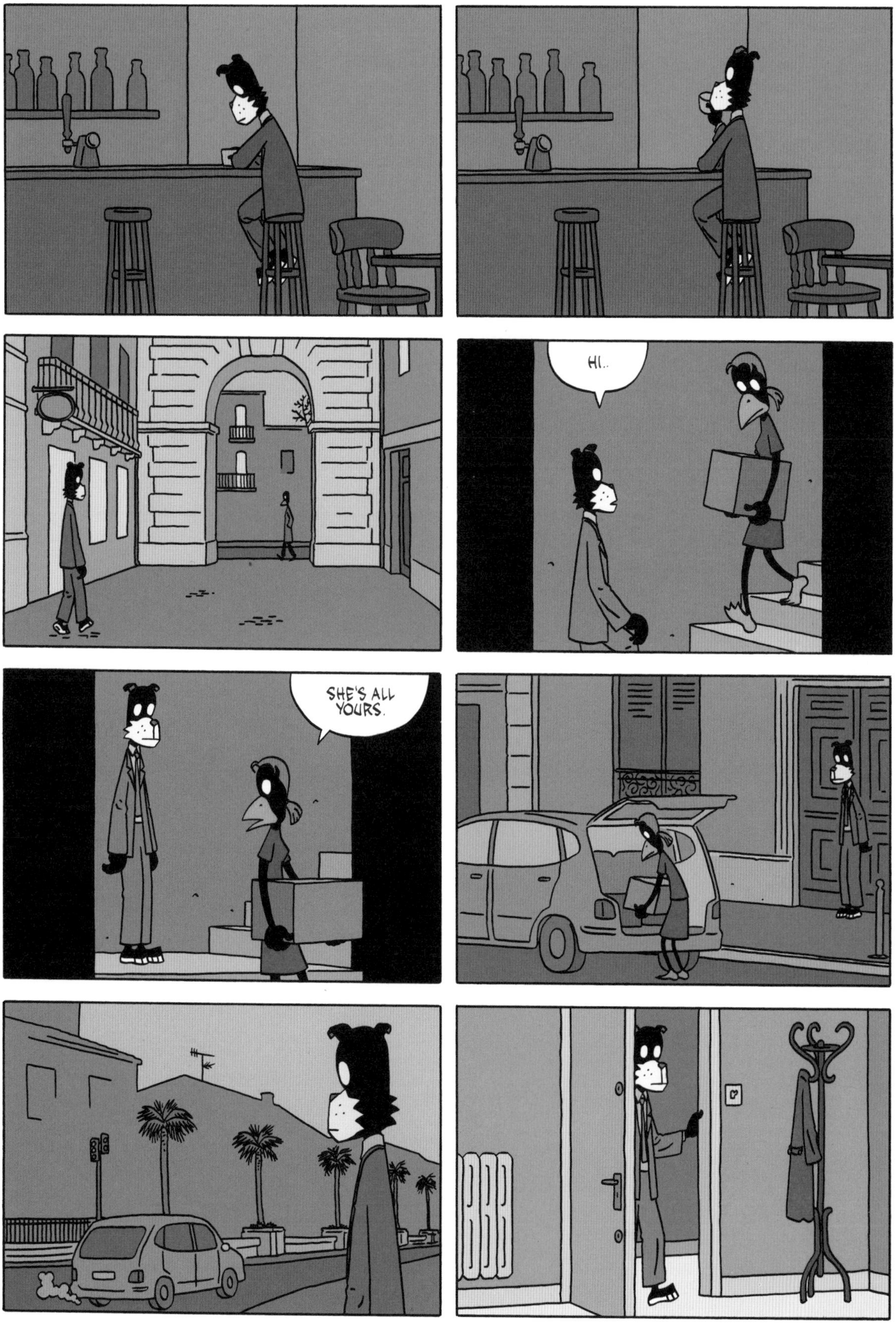
HI..
SHE'S ALL YOURS.

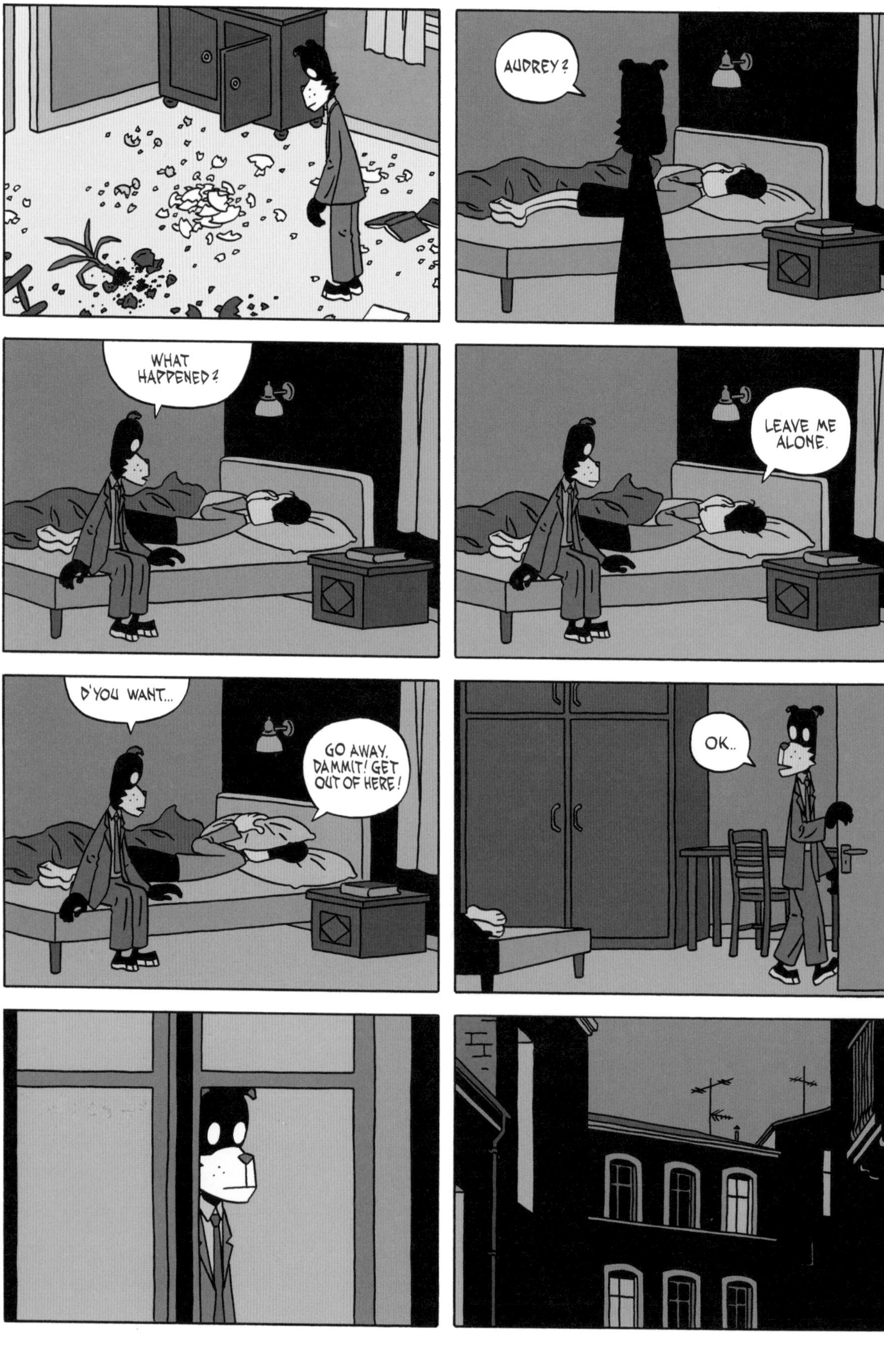
AUDREY?
WHAT HAPPENED?
LEAVE ME ALONE.
D'YOU WANT...
GO AWAY, DAMMIT! GET OUT OF HERE!
OK..

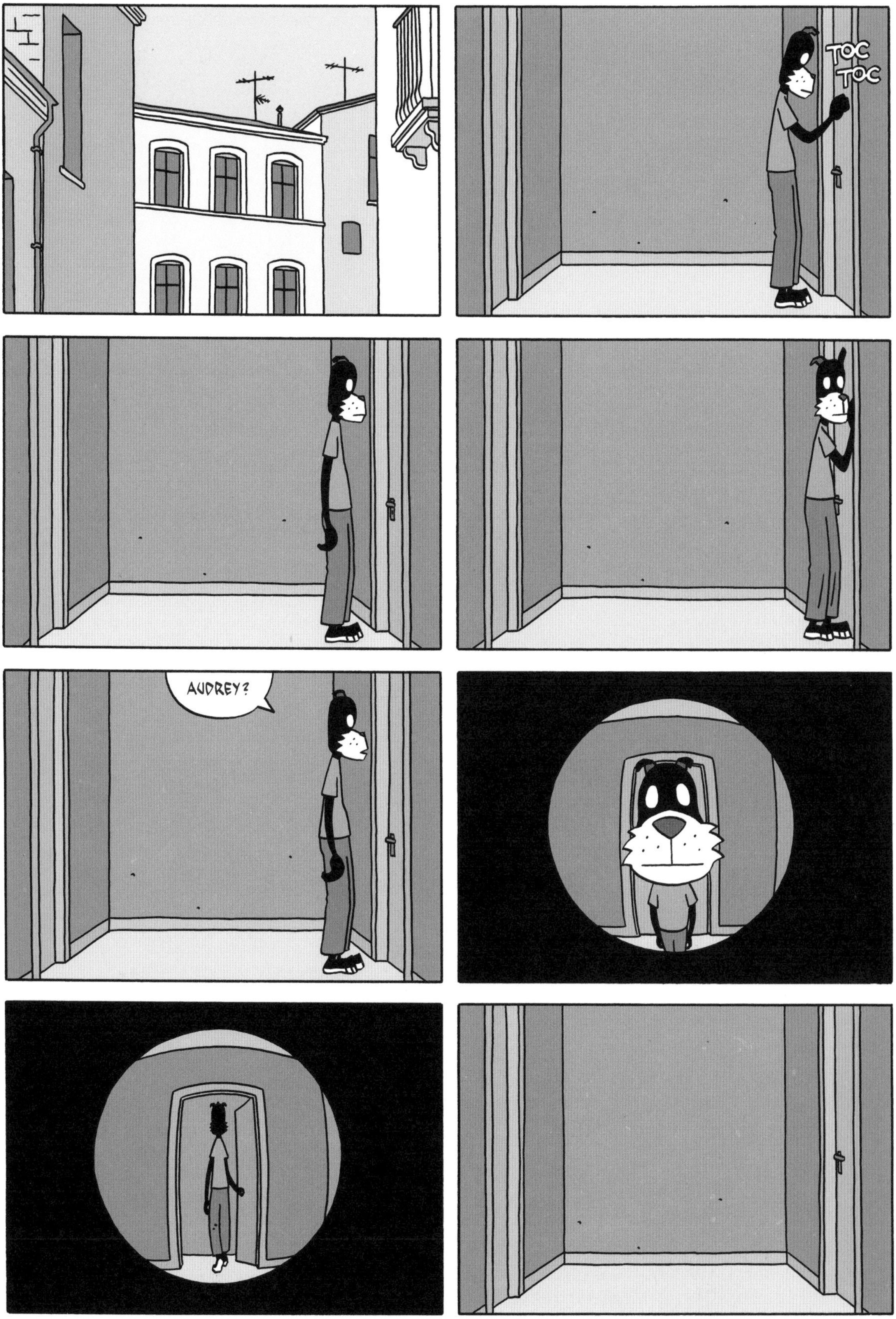
TOC
TOC
AUDREY?

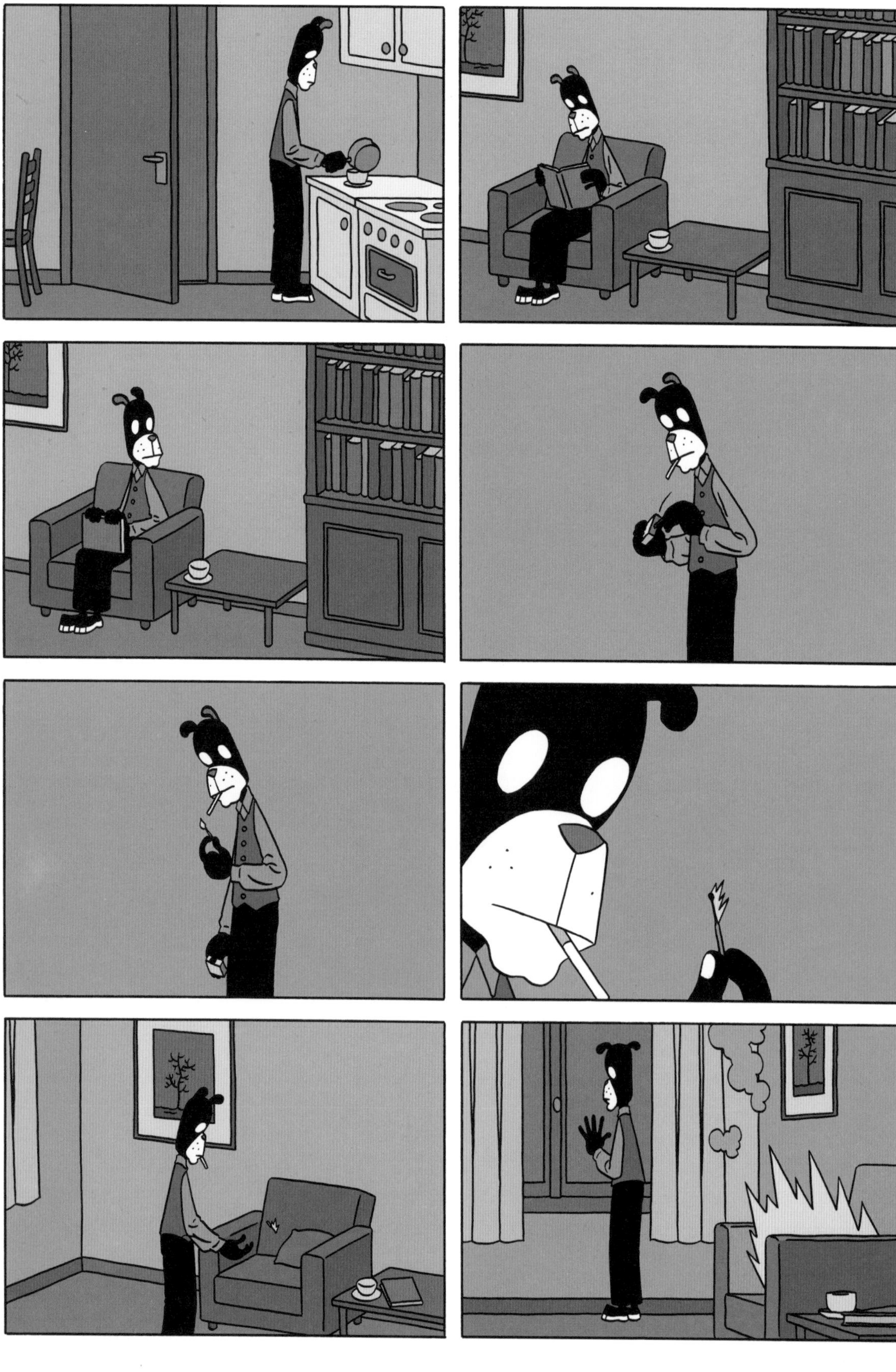

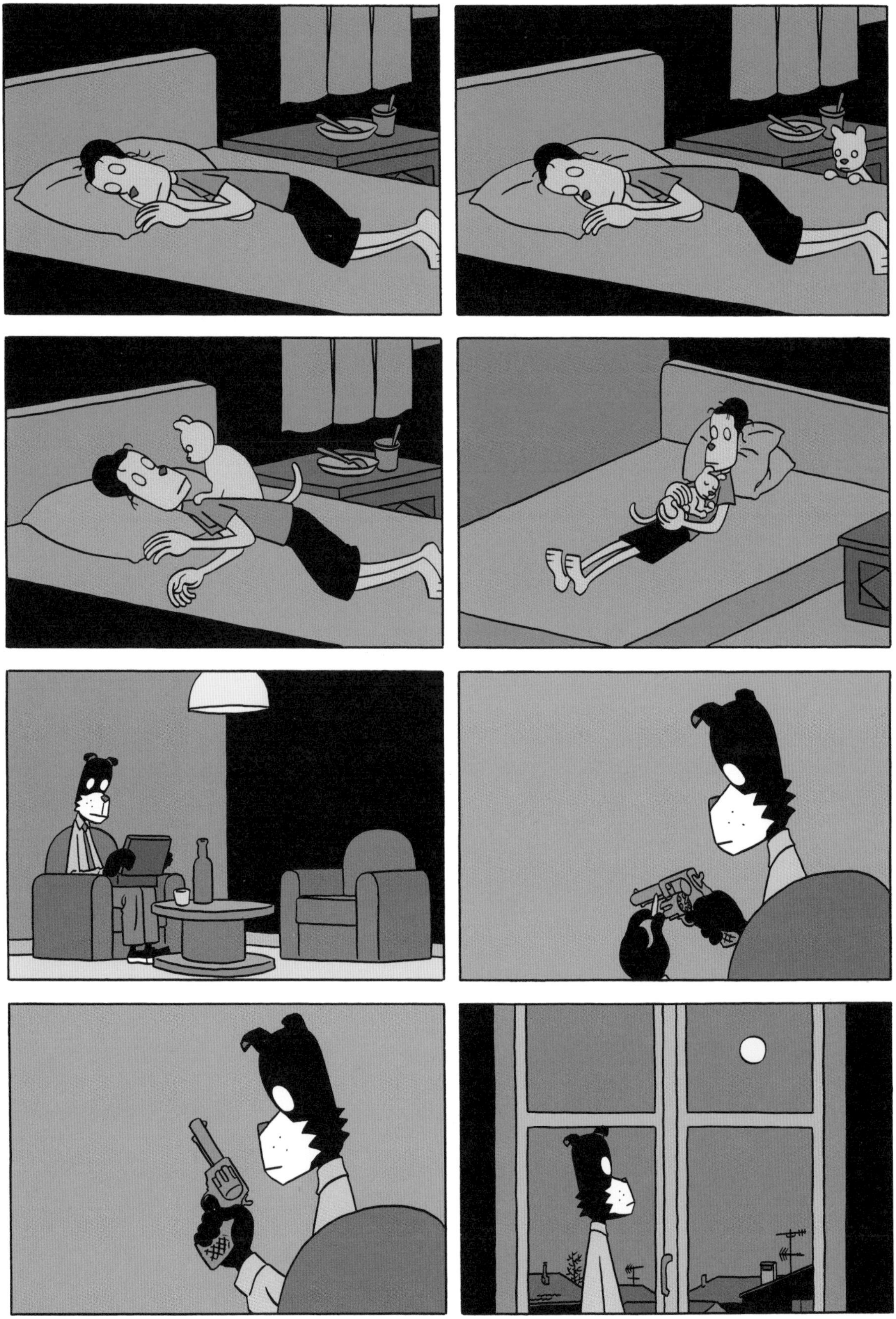

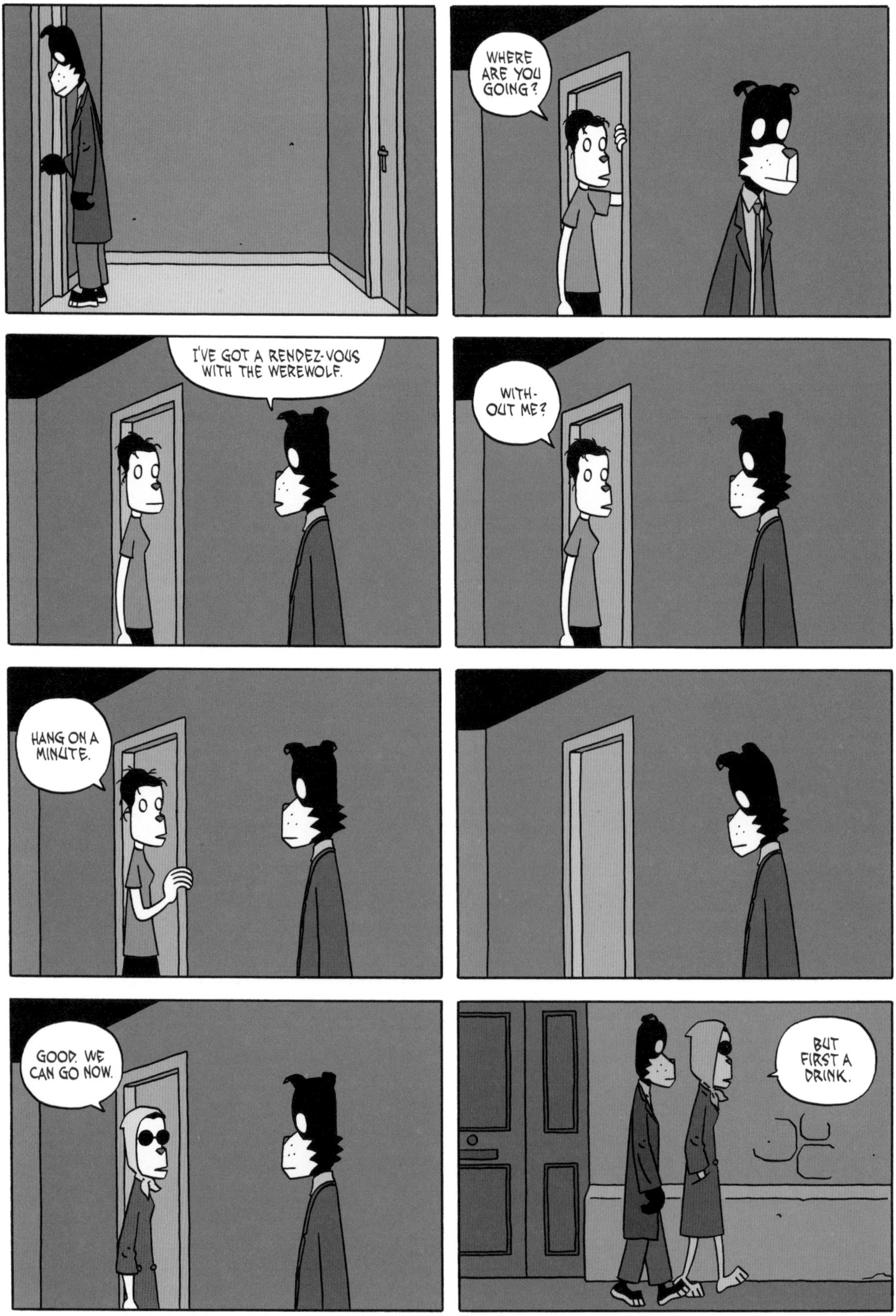
WHERE ARE YOU GOING?
I'VE GOT A RENDEZ-VOUS WITH THE WEREWOLF.
WITH-OUT ME?
HANG ON A MINUTE.
GOOD. WE CAN GO NOW.
BUT FIRST A DRINK.

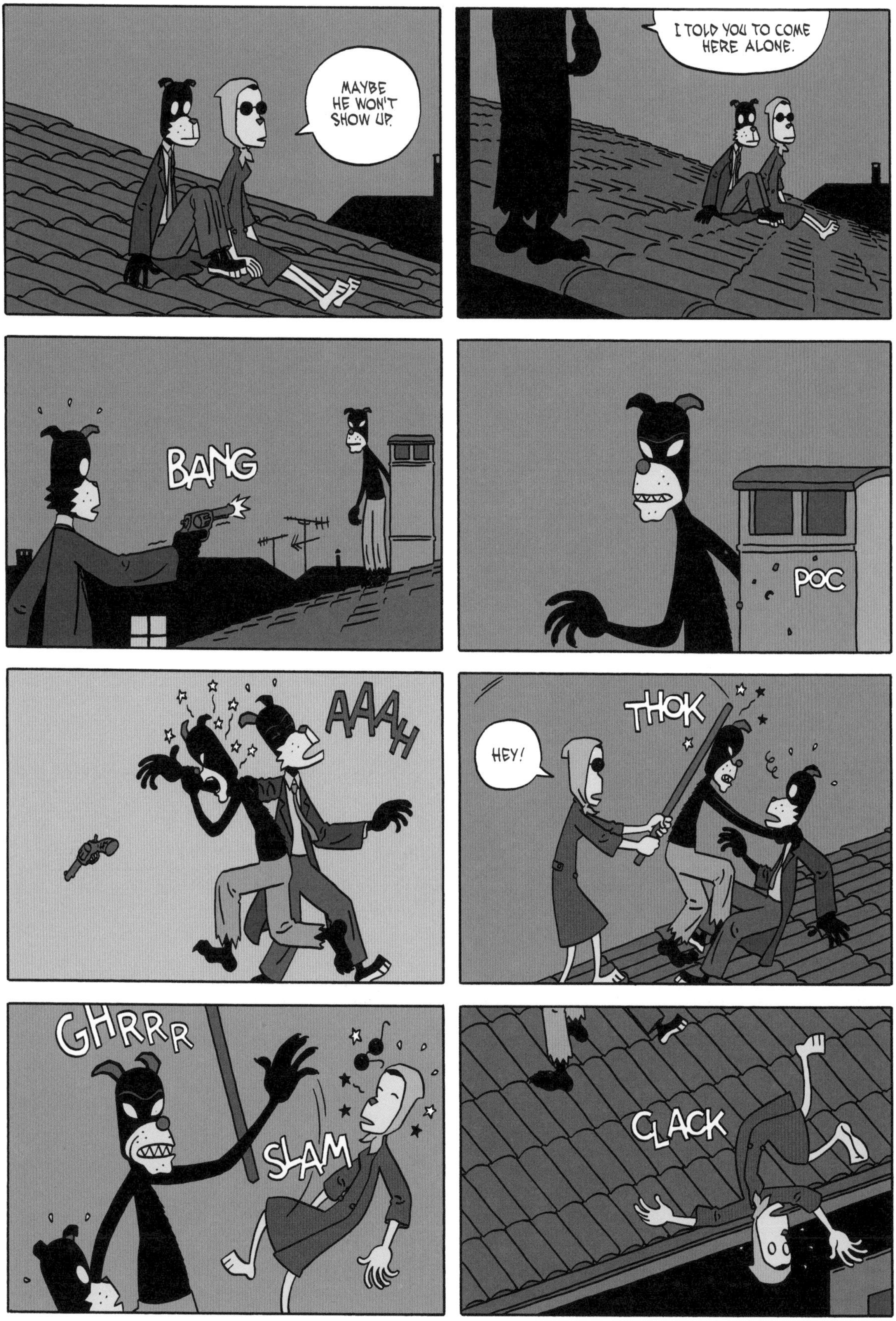
MAYBE HE WON'T SHOW UP.
I TOLD YOU TO COME HERE ALONE.
BANG
POC
AAAAH
HEY!
THOK
GHRRRR
SLAM
CLACK

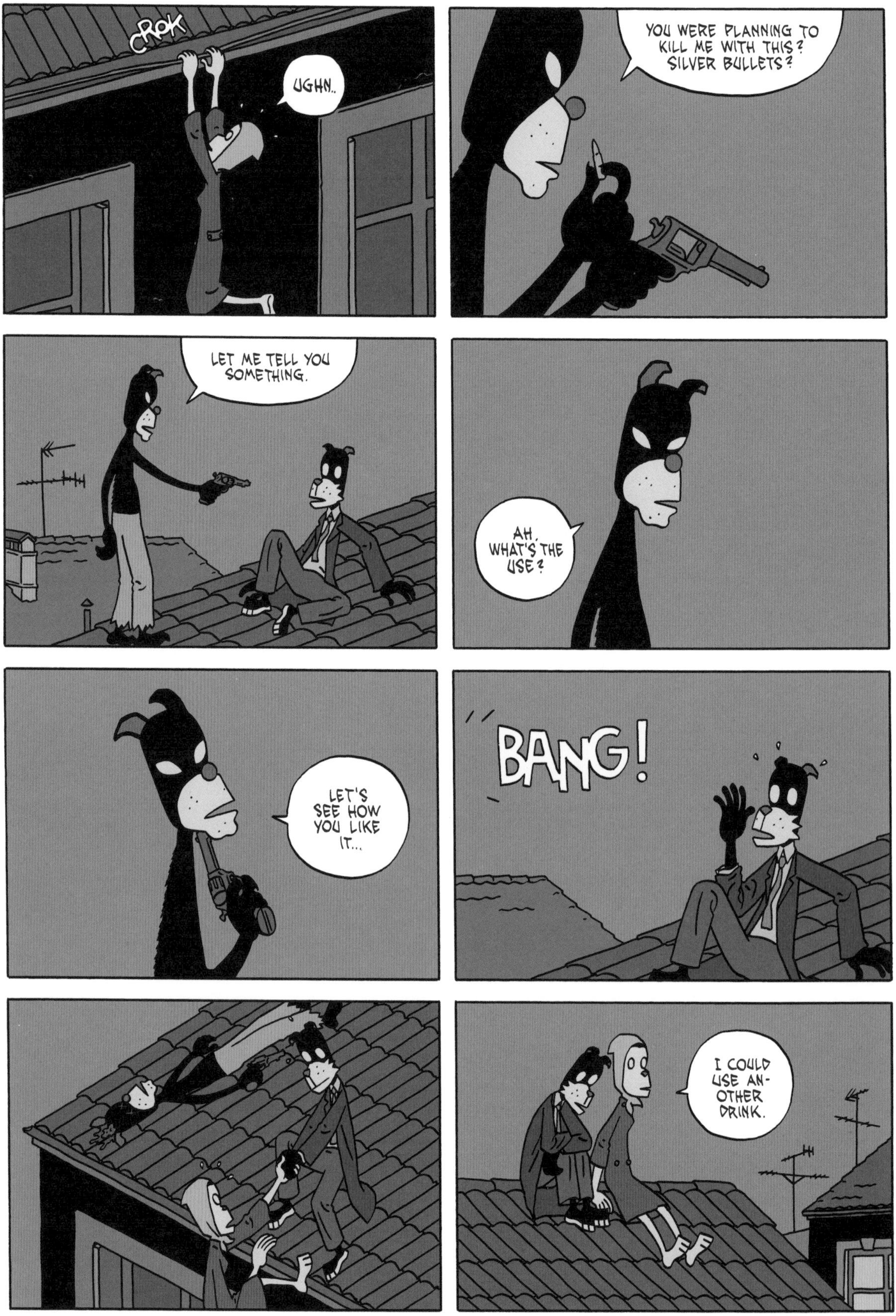
CROK
UGHN..
YOU WERE PLANNING TO KILL ME WITH THIS? SILVER BULLETS?
LET ME TELL YOU SOMETHING.
AH, WHAT'S THE USE?
LET'S SEE HOW YOU LIKE IT...
BANG!
I COULD USE AN-OTHER DRINK.

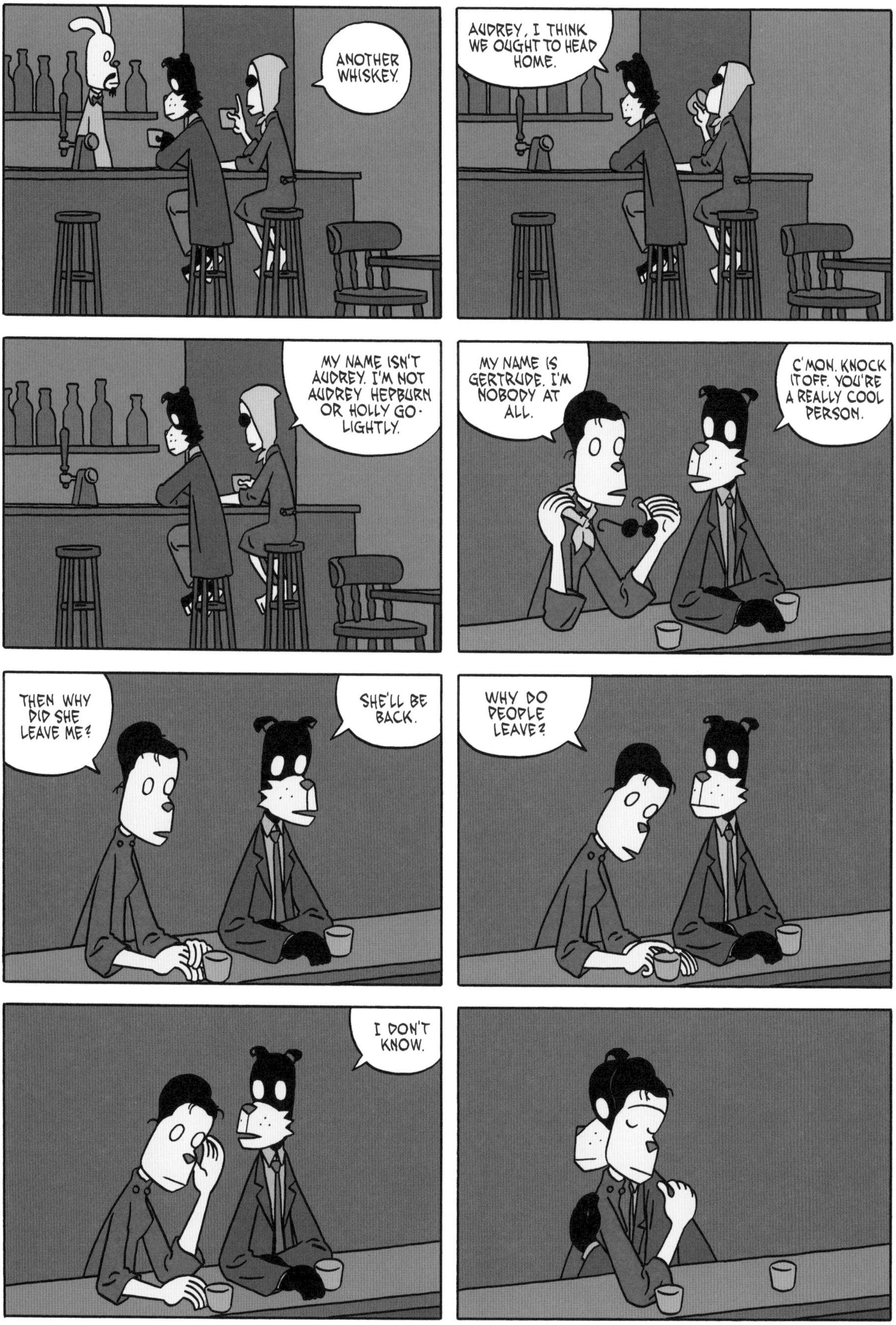
ANOTHER WHISKEY.
AUDREY, I THINK WE OUGHT TO HEAD HOME.
MY NAME ISN'T AUDREY. I'M NOT AUDREY HEPBURN OR HOLLY GO-LIGHTLY.
MY NAME IS GERTRUDE. I'M NOBODY AT ALL.
C'MON. KNOCK IT OFF. YOU'RE A REALLY COOL PERSON.
THEN WHY DID SHE LEAVE ME?
SHE'LL BE BACK.
WHY DO PEOPLE LEAVE?
I DON'T KNOW.

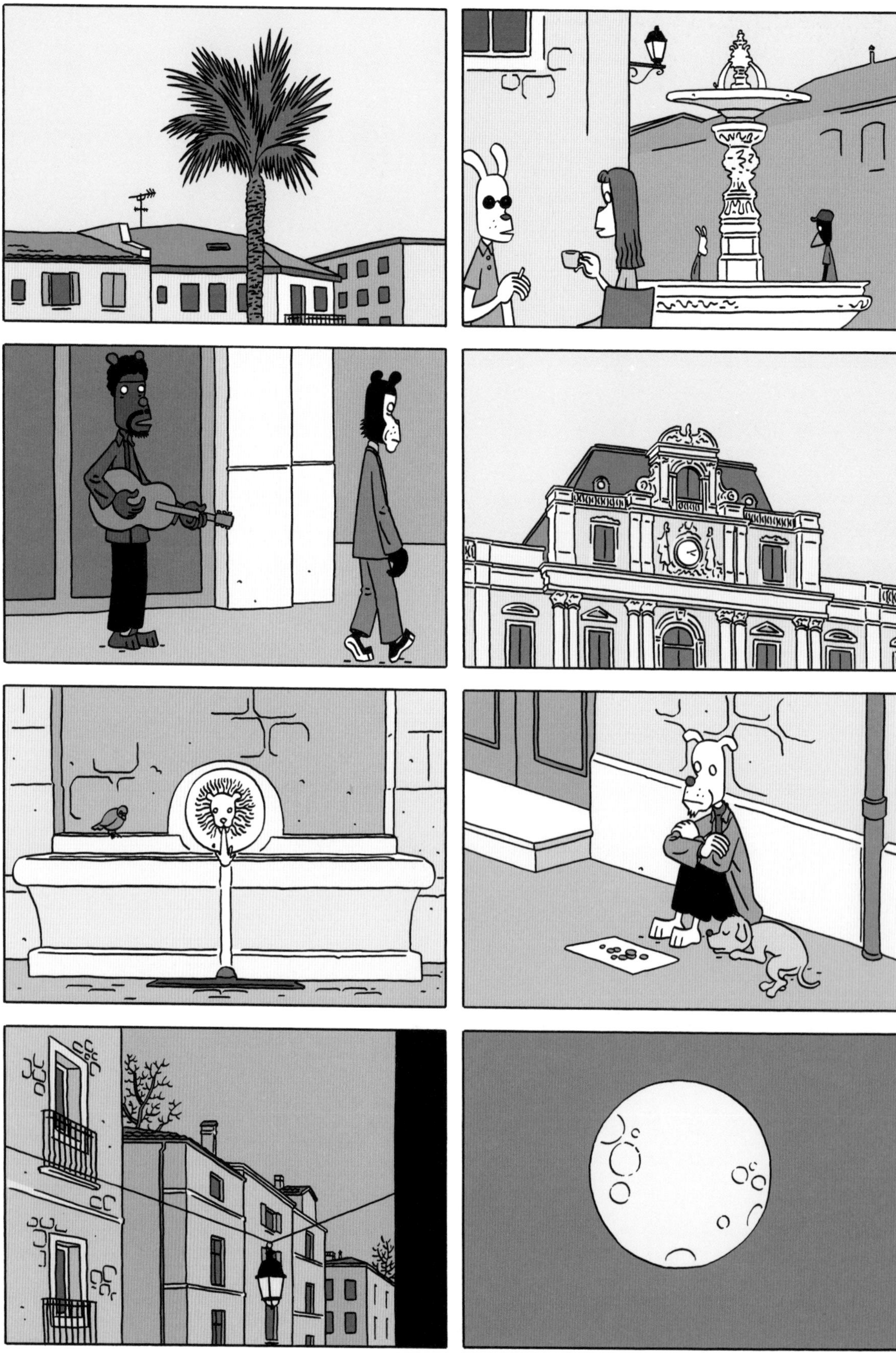

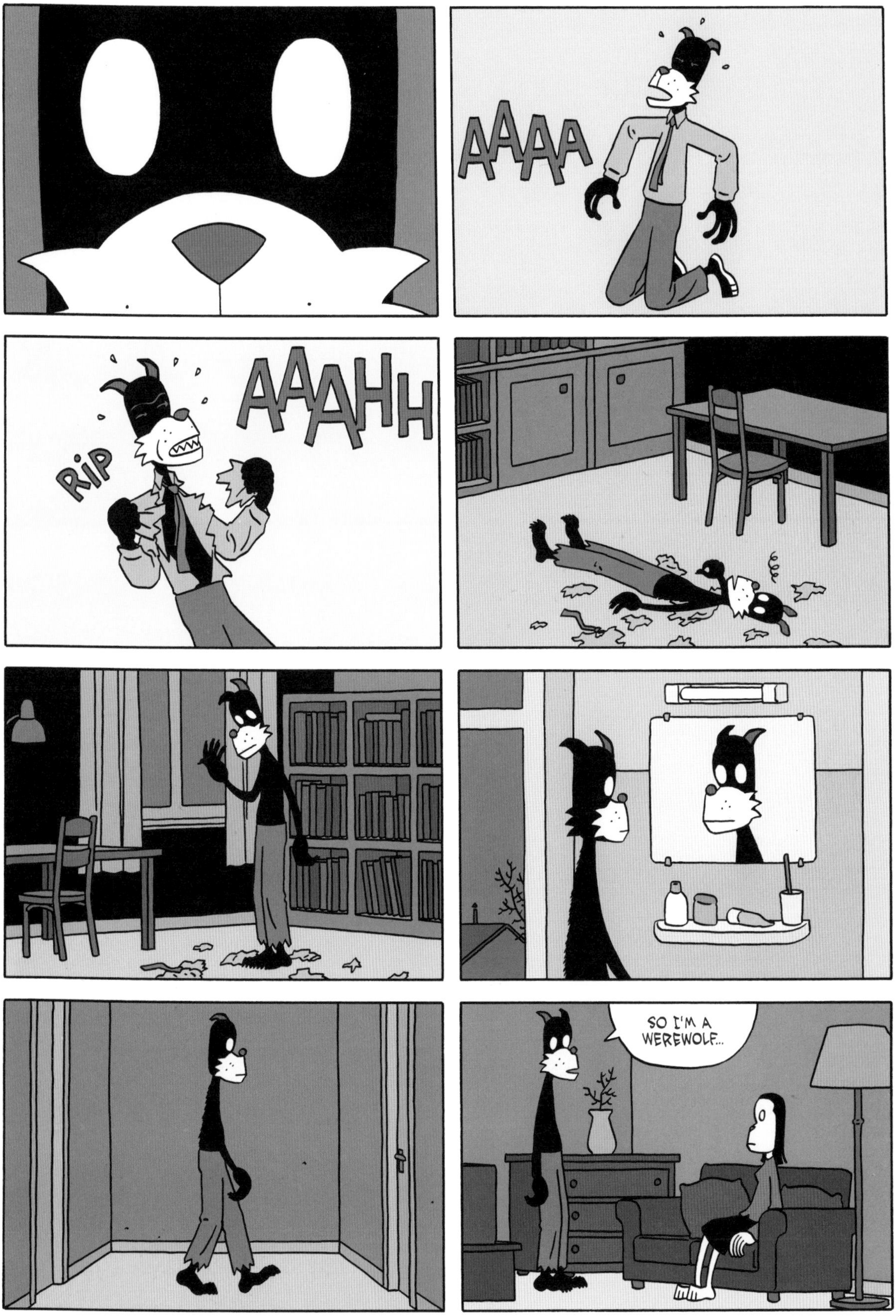
AAAA
RIP
AAAHH
SO I'M A WEREWOLF...

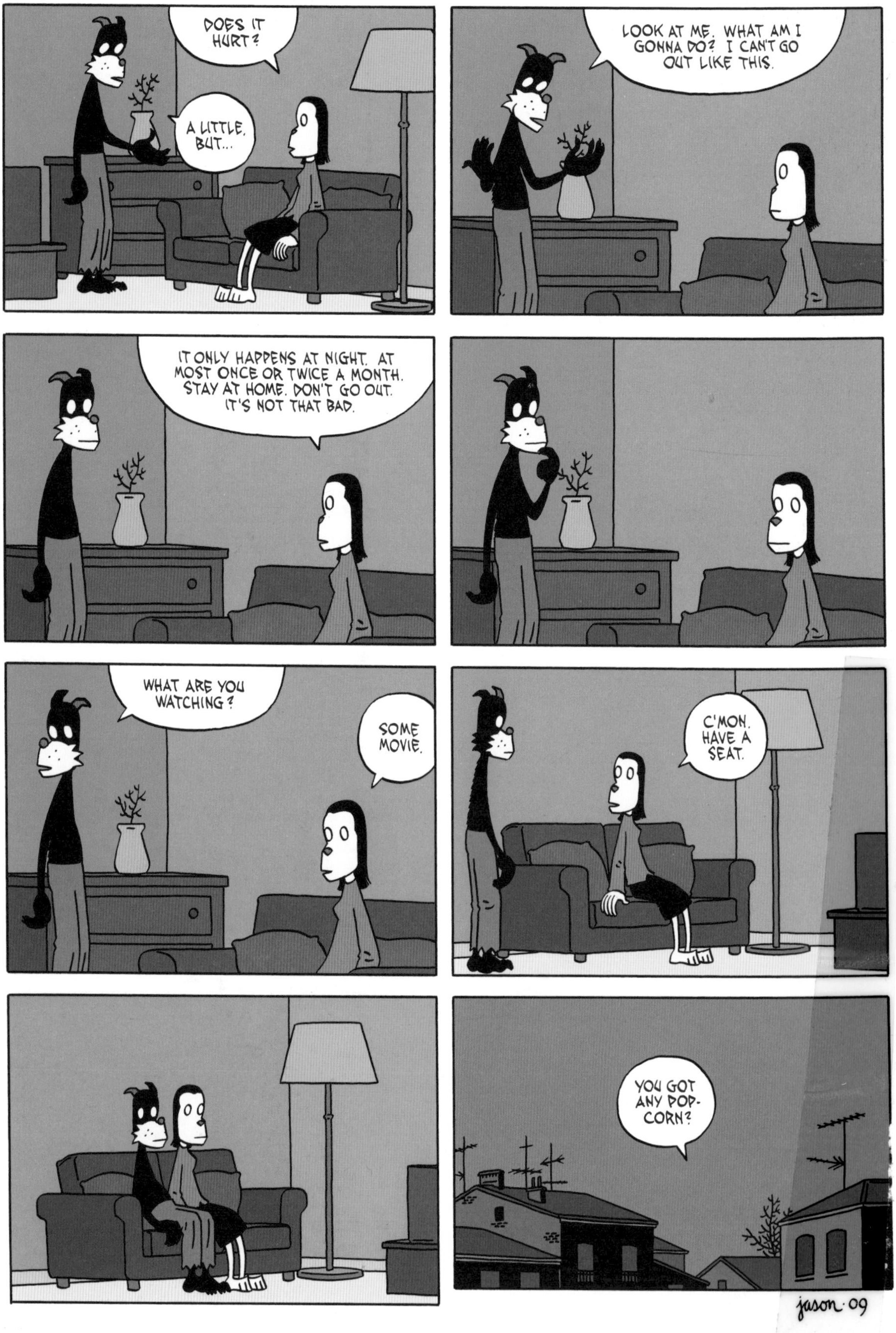
DOES IT HURT?
A LITTLE, BUT...
LOOK AT ME. WHAT AM I GONNA DO? I CAN'T GO OUT LIKE THIS.
IT ONLY HAPPENS AT NIGHT. AT MOST ONCE OR TWICE A MONTH. STAY AT HOME. DON'T GO OUT. IT'S NOT THAT BAD.
WHAT ARE YOU WATCHING?
SOME MOVIE.
C'MON. HAVE A SEAT.
YOU GOT ANY POP-CORN?
jason·09